T0146973

An Analysis of

Immanuel Kant's

Religion within the Boundaries of Mere Reason

Ian Jackson

Published by Macat International Ltd
24:13 Coda Centre, 189 Munster Road, London SW6 6AW.

Distributed exclusively by Routledge
2 Park Square, Milton Park, Abingdon, Oxon OX14 4RN
711 Third Avenue, New York, NY 10017, USA

Routledge is an imprint of the Taylor & Francis Group, an informa business

www.macat.com
info@macat.com

Cataloguing in Publication Data
A catalogue record for this book is available from the British Library.
Library of Congress Cataloguing-in-Publication Data is available upon request.
Cover illustration: Etienne Gilfillan

ISBN 978-1-912303-02-1 (hardback)
ISBN 978-1-912128-62-4 (paperback)
ISBN 978-1-912281-90-9 (e-book)

Notice
The information in this book is designed to orientate readers of the work under analysis,
to elucidate and contextualise its key ideas and themes, and to aid in the development
of critical thinking skills. It is not meant to be used, nor should it be used, as a
substitute for original thinking or in place of original writing or research. References and
notes are provided for informational purposes and their presence does not constitute
endorsement of the information or opinions therein. This book is presented solely for
educational purposes. It is sold on the understanding that the publisher is not engaged
to provide any scholarly advice. The publisher has made every effort to ensure that
this book is accurate and up-to-date, but makes no warranties or representations with
regard to the completeness or reliability of the information it contains. The information
and the opinions provided herein are not guaranteed or warranted to produce particular
results and may not be suitable for students of every ability. The publisher shall not be
liable for any loss, damage or disruption arising from any errors or omissions, or from
the use of this book, including, but not limited to, special, incidental, consequential or
other damages caused, or alleged to have been caused, directly or indirectly, by the
information contained within.

CONTENTS

WAYS IN TO THE TEXT

Who Was Immanuel Kant? — 9

What Does *Religion within the Boundaries of Mere Reason* Say? — 10

Why Does *Religion within the Boundaries of Mere Reason* Matter? — 12

SECTION 1: INFLUENCES

Module 1: The Author and the Historical Context — 16

Module 2: Academic Context — 20

Module 3: The Problem — 24

Module 4: The Author's Contribution — 29

SECTION 2: IDEAS

Module 5: Main Ideas — 35

Module 6: Secondary Ideas — 40

Module 7: Achievement — 45

Module 8: Place in the Author's Work — 50

SECTION 3: IMPACT

Module 9: The First Responses — 56

Module 10: The Evolving Debate — 61

Module 11: Impact and Influence Today — 66

Module 12: Where Next? — 71

Glossary of Terms — 76

People Mentioned in the Text — 84

Works Cited — 92

THE MACAT LIBRARY

The Macat Library is a series of unique academic explorations of seminal works in the humanities and social sciences – books and papers that have had a significant and widely recognised impact on their disciplines. It has been created to serve as much more than just a summary of what lies between the covers of a great book. It illuminates and explores the influences on, ideas of, and impact of that book. Our goal is to offer a learning resource that encourages critical thinking and fosters a better, deeper understanding of important ideas.

Each publication is divided into three Sections: Influences, Ideas, and Impact. Each Section has four Modules. These explore every important facet of the work, and the responses to it.

This Section-Module structure makes a Macat Library book easy to use, but it has another important feature. Because each Macat book is written to the same format, it is possible (and encouraged!) to cross-reference multiple Macat books along the same lines of inquiry or research. This allows the reader to open up interesting interdisciplinary pathways.

To further aid your reading, lists of glossary terms and people mentioned are included at the end of this book (these are indicated by an asterisk [*] throughout) – as well as a list of works cited.

Macat has worked with the University of Cambridge to identify the elements of critical thinking and understand the ways in which six different skills combine to enable effective thinking.
Three allow us to fully understand a problem; three more give us the tools to solve it. Together, these six skills make up the **PACIER** model of critical thinking. They are:

ANALYSIS – understanding how an argument is built
EVALUATION – exploring the strengths and weaknesses of an argument
INTERPRETATION – understanding issues of meaning

CREATIVE THINKING – coming up with new ideas and fresh connections
PROBLEM-SOLVING – producing strong solutions
REASONING – creating strong arguments

To find out more, visit **WWW.MACAT.COM.**

CRITICAL THINKING AND *RELIGION WITHIN THE BOUNDARIES OF MERE REASON*

Primary critical thinking skill: REASONING
Secondary critical thinking skill: CREATIVE THINKING

The eighteenth-century philosopher Immanuel Kant is as daunting as he is influential: widely considered to be not only one of the most challenging thinkers of all time, but also one of the most important. His *Religion Within the Boundaries of Mere Reason* takes on two of his central preoccupations – the reasoning powers of the human mind, and religion – and applies the full force of his reasoning abilities to consider the relationship between them.

In critical thinking, reasoning is all about constructing arguments: arguments that are persuasive, systematic, comprehensive, and well-evidenced. And any examination of involves stripping reasoning back to its barest essentials and attempting to get at the nature of the world by asking what we can know about God and morality from the power of our minds alone. Beginning from the axiom that God is, by definition, unknowable, Kant reasons that it is humans who bear the responsibility of creating the Kingdom of God. This, he suggests, we can do by acting morally in the world we experience – with a morality that can be shaped by reason alone.

Dense and challenging, but closely and persuasively reasoned, Kant's case for human responsibility shows reasoning skills at their most impressive.

ABOUT THE AUTHOR OF THE ORIGINAL WORK

Immanuel Kant, the man who changed the way the world thinks about thoughts, lived a singularly uneventful life. Born in 1724 in the Prussian city of Königsberg (now Kaliningrad, Russia), Kant rarely left his hometown. He taught at the local university and wrote. He never married, and died in Königsberg in 1804. But his many insightful philosophical works brought him widespread fame in his lifetime, and he continues to be regarded as one of the world's greatest philosophers.

ABOUT THE AUTHOR OF THE ANALYSIS

Ian Jackson is a PhD student in the Politics, Philosophy and Religion department at Lancaster University. He is interested in the role new media plays in the dissemination of ideas.

ABOUT MACAT

GREAT WORKS FOR CRITICAL THINKING

Macat is focused on making the ideas of the world's great thinkers accessible and comprehensible to everybody, everywhere, in ways that promote the development of enhanced critical thinking skills.

It works with leading academics from the world's top universities to produce new analyses that focus on the ideas and the impact of the most influential works ever written across a wide variety of academic disciplines. Each of the works that sit at the heart of its growing library is an enduring example of great thinking. But by setting them in context – and looking at the influences that shaped their authors, as well as the responses they provoked – Macat encourages readers to look at these classics and game-changers with fresh eyes. Readers learn to think, engage and challenge their ideas, rather than simply accepting them.

'Macat offers an amazing first-of-its-kind tool for interdisciplinary learning and research. Its focus on works that transformed their disciplines and its rigorous approach, drawing on the world's leading experts and educational institutions, opens up a world-class education to anyone.'

Andreas Schleicher
Director for Education and Skills, Organisation for Economic Co-operation and Development

'Macat is taking on some of the major challenges in university education … They have drawn together a strong team of active academics who are producing teaching materials that are novel in the breadth of their approach.'

Prof Lord Broers,
former Vice-Chancellor of the University of Cambridge

'The Macat vision is exceptionally exciting. It focuses upon new modes of learning which analyse and explain seminal texts which have profoundly influenced world thinking and so social and economic development. It promotes the kind of critical thinking which is essential for any society and economy.
This is the learning of the future.'

Rt Hon Charles Clarke, former UK Secretary of State for Education

'The Macat analyses provide immediate access to the critical conversation surrounding the books that have shaped their respective discipline, which will make them an invaluable resource to all of those, students and teachers, working in the field.'

Professor William Tronzo, University of California at San Diego

WAYS IN TO THE TEXT

KEY POINTS

- The German philosopher Immanuel Kant was born in 1724.
- In *Religion within the Boundaries of Mere Reason*, Kant set out to examine where reason and faith intersect and where they diverge.
- The text was not simply a theological exercise; Kant intended it to be a political text in response to King Friedrich Wilhelm II's* enforcement of religious orthodoxy.

Who Was Immanuel Kant?

Immanuel Kant, the author of *Religion within the Boundaries of Mere Reason* (1793), was born in 1724 in Königsberg,* a city on the Baltic Sea in Prussia*—a state that today forms part of northern Germany. Religion was an important aspect of his early life. Kant and his family were followers of the Protestant branch of the Christian faith; specifically, they were Pietists,* members of a reform effort that began in the seventeenth century and which asked individuals to focus on an inner religious experience. Pietism stressed the role of moral conscience and enforced a literal interpretation of the Bible.

Kant's father was a harness-maker. From 1732, when Immanuel was eight years old, he attended the Collegium Fridericianum in Königsberg, a Pietist private school. The school's patron was the

Prussian king Friedrich Wilhelm I.* In 1740, at just 16 years old, Kant enrolled at the University of Königsberg, where he would remain for the rest of his career. His tutor, the philosopher Martin Knutzen,* seems to have had a profound effect on the young Kant. He introduced him to the mathematics of the English physicist Isaac Newton* and the thinking of the German philosophers Gottfried Leibniz* and Christian Wolff.* He also seems to have attempted to dissuade Kant from following idealism,* the philosophical position which holds that reality, as we comprehend it, is a mental construct; Kant, however, was to become synonymous with this school of thought.

The death of his father in 1746 forced Kant to work as a private tutor. While this disrupted his studies, he managed to publish his first philosophical work in 1747. This work, *Thoughts on the True Estimation of Living Forces,*[1] marked Kant as a young scholar of extraordinary talent.

What Does *Religion* Say?

Kant's 1793 work *Religion within the Boundaries of Mere Reason* principally deals with theology* (the systematic study of religious ideas such as the nature of God), philosophy of religion* (use of philosophical thought to either confirm or deny the existence of a divine being), ethics* (the area of philosophy dealing with questions of morality and "right" action), and metaphysics* (the branch of philosophy addressing questions concerning the nature of existence). The text answers a question Kant posed at the end of an earlier work. In *Critique of Pure Reason,*[2] published a dozen years earlier, Kant asked: What can I know? What ought I to do? And also, what may I hope? That last question takes center stage in *Religion*.

Kant saw these as fundamental aspects of human reason. But the question "What may I hope?" remained problematic for two reasons. First, "hope" lies in the domain of religion and theology. These fields confront ideas that remain impossible to prove: God's existence and the nature of the soul. But unprovable ideas did not mesh with Kant's previous body of work. He had spent his career dealing in ideas that science or philosophy might confirm. In *Religion*, Kant attempts to address—at least in part—areas that these disciplines could not explain.

In his earlier works, Kant had avoided a direct confrontation with theology. His decision to discuss the Bible and Christian theology surprised many of his contemporaries. He engaged with this material in some measure as a protest against the authority wielded by political institutions on religious matters. Although linking freedom of religious expression and skepticism of Church authority was controversial at the time, Kant felt compelled to make these arguments to assert his right to freedom of expression. While Kant was not directly censored, he was subsequently contacted by the king (through an intermediary) and he agreed to refrain from writing or lecturing about religion again. He kept that promise until the king's death in 1797.

In *Religion*, though, Kant attacked theology. He argued that morality stems from reason and the autonomy of the individual agent—that is, the capacity of every individual to act independently. He maintained that religious ideas held no more validity in terms of teaching morality than unassisted thought. And he asserted that before religious ideas could be accepted, they would have to pass the test of human reason. But while Kant advocated the autonomy of human beings, religious ideas of evil, grace* (the unlimited favor and forgiveness of God), and providence* (the care and guidance offered by God) seem to have been important to him.

While not as influential as Kant's earlier *Critiques*,*³ *Religion* remains an important text. If it were simply an attack on the laws and institutions of his time, it would be of limited interest today. But tensions within the work still capture our attention. At its core is a battle between Enlightenment* ideas—ideas grounded in the rational current of seventeenth- and eighteenth-century thought known as the Enlightenment—and political and religious authorities. More than three centuries later, this battle continues to rage in some parts of the world.

The text's relevance to theology is, paradoxically, more ambiguous. Kant believed that God was unknowable—but that does not mean God was unnecessary. In fact, Kant argued that human beings do require both God and grace. But he diverged from traditional Church teaching about what "God" and "grace" really mean. Kant intended *Religion* to reclaim theological concepts and doctrines through the intermediating power of reason. But he may also have used it to demonstrate how moral philosophy* requires theological work. In this way, the book combines two separate academic fields. The ambiguity of this combination is clearly visible in the work of Kant's followers.

However one interprets it, *Religion* is at its heart a work like any other work by Kant: the way he thinks about things is as important as the conclusions he reaches. He attempts to domesticate religion by subjecting truths to reason.

Why Does *Religion* Matter?

More than 200 years after its publication, *Religion* continues to influence debates within philosophy and theology. Yet it does not stand alone in Kant's body of work. His earlier writing on religion provides an important theoretical framework for this later book.

Two features deserve particular attention. First, Kant believed that it was impossible for human beings to fully understand certain bodies and objects such as God, the soul, or the cosmos. Second, he argued that morality required beliefs in God and the immortality of the soul.

Here lies an important contradiction. Although he was suspicious of the institutions of religion and their claims of absolute truth, Kant still saw religion as essential. Kant's complex and ambiguous relation to religion remains an important area of study today. He raises the powerful idea that theoretical concepts of theology have a practical or moral necessity. In essence, according to Kant, humanity needs God—whether or not we can prove His existence. This ambiguity has won *Religion* both praise and criticism.

Kant saw human reason as the ultimate authority in philosophy, ethics, and religion. The Scottish philosopher David Hume,* roughly a contemporary of Kant, had also launched attacks on natural theology. Where Hume took a negative and critical approach, Kant instead justified religious concepts by making them products of pure practical reason. In doing so, he opened up new philosophical means for approaching religious topics. Kant asserted the autonomy of philosophy and the authority of reason, but he fenced them in. Philosophy prevailed in matters of methodology and epistemology*—the nature and scope of knowledge.

Theology, in Kant's view, existed outside these fields. Kant played a significant role in shaping the future study of theology and philosophy, and his work helped to create a new field of study: the philosophy of religion. *Religion* played an important part in this. It continued Kant's effort to use philosophy in ways other than as an aid to a revelation-based theology* (one based on communication with a divine being). Instead, Kant wanted to examine the role played by religious concepts within the economy of human reason.

Kant insisted that theological and religious doctrines depended on morality. Most other thinkers in his day (and some in our own) believed the exact opposite. The way in which Kant related theology, religious scripture, and reason in *Religion* remains controversial and continues to fuel complex debates about Kant's philosophy of religion. These debates focus on the relationship between theology and philosophy as intellectual endeavors and institutional realities.

NOTES

1 Immanuel Kant, *Thoughts on the True Estimation of Living Forces*, in Cambridge Edition of the Works of Immanuel Kant (Cambridge: Cambridge University Press, 2012), 1–155.

2 Immanuel Kant, *Critique of Pure Reason*, trans. Paul Guyer and Allen Wood (Cambridge: Cambridge University Press, 1999).

3 Immanuel Kant, *Critique of Practical Reason, Critique of Pure Reason, Critique on the Power of Judgment.*

SECTION 1
INFLUENCES

THE AUTHOR AND THE HISTORICAL CONTEXT

KEY POINTS

- One of Kant's more mature works, *Religion within the Boundaries of Mere Reason* contains ideas that have now achieved widespread—if not universal—acceptance.

- Kant's family practiced Pietism,* an offshoot of Lutheran* Protestantism.* His early life was dominated by religion.

- Kant was deeply influenced by the intellectual and cultural movements known as the Enlightenment* and rationalism,* both of which emphasized rational thought over superstition and religion—and both of which the king of Kant's native Prussia, Friedrich Wilhelm II,* sought to suppress.

Why Read This Text?

Religion within the Boundaries of Mere Reason (1793) offers Immanuel Kant's most sustained treatment of religious and theological topics. It is also one of his most mature works. The choice of title itself signals Kant's attitude and approach to the subject. Christianity had traditionally relied on two things to sustain its claims: faith and scripture* (that is, holy texts). But Kant held that religious themes and doctrines must survive the scrutiny of human reason. In other words, he attempted to evaluate religious ideas using a strict set of guidelines. These guidelines disregarded anything that could not be logically— and perhaps even scientifically—explained. Such an approach was not simply novel in 1793, when Kant wrote the work. It was truly groundbreaking.

> 66 [We] can call this ground a natural propensity to evil, and, since it must nevertheless always come about through one's own fault, we can further even call it a *radical* innate *evil* in human nature (not any the less brought upon us by ourselves.) 99
>
> Immanuel Kant, *Religion and Rational Philosophy*

We may see the thoughts Kant developed in *Religion* as a continuation of a process begun earlier, especially in his *Critiques*.[*1] While these works present his fully developed philosophical system, they touch only briefly on religious themes. Still, they unfailingly focus on a single core concept—that religious faith must be a rational, moral faith. Kant meant two things by this: first, that faith must emerge from an individual's commitment to following practical laws prescribed by reason; and second, that moral law cannot be derived from religious commitments that do not stand up to the scrutiny of reason. In the eighteenth century, society and the law treated morality and truth as the province of religion. So in deciding to examine these ideas in *Religion*, Kant made a significant—and bold—move.

In the twentieth century, scholars paid less attention to *Religion* than to Kant's other major critical works, but the central themes it addresses, especially about the nature of the will, remain central to critical practical philosophy. Scholars disagree on *Religion*. Some feel it contains crucial developments of Kant's moral philosophy.[*] Others believe it simply applies pre-established conceptions to the field of theology—in which case, its principal importance depends on one's attitude to theology.

Author's Life
Kant was born in 1724 in the town of Königsberg.[*] Now part of northern Germany, in Kant's day it belonged to Prussia.[*] His father worked as a harness-maker.

Religion dominated Kant's early life. His family identified with the Pietist movement, a strict form of Lutheranism—a branch of Protestant Christianity founded on the theology of Martin Luther.* Originating in the seventeenth century, Pietism stressed personal faith, inner religious experience, and the role of moral conscience. Scholars still debate the extent to which his Pietistic education influenced Kant's philosophy of religion* (the use of philosophical thought to either prove or disprove the existence of a divine being). And even among those who believe it did, there was disagreement about whether that influence was positive or negative. But the mature Kant clearly rejected the Pietist belief in the literal truth of the Bible. Indeed, in *Religion*, Kant argued that over the theology of the Bible there stood on the side of the sciences a "philosophical theology … a property held in trust by another faculty."[2] In Kant's view, that property was "reason."

Kant received an excellent education for his time. In 1732, he enrolled at the Collegium Fridericianum, a private school that catered to the Königsberg Pietist community. Eight years later—at only 16 years old—he began his studies at the University of Königsberg. He would remain there throughout his career.

Author's Background

Kant wrote the essays comprising *Religion* while working as professor of logic and metaphysics at the University of Königsberg. The complete work was first made available during the Easter fair of 1793.

Kant strongly aligned himself with the rational principles of the Enlightenment and, during the time he wrote *Religion*, he saw these principles at risk both at home and abroad. The Enlightenment had fed revolutionary sentiment in France. Kant was been an outspoken defender of the movement, which would culminate in the French Revolution* of 1789–99. This was a period of intense political turbulence—in the course of which France's king was executed and a republic instituted—that was to influence the course of modern history.

While the upheaval in France had very little direct effect on Prussia, the conservative government of King Friedrich Wilhelm II feared that Enlightenment thought and the philosophy of rationalism (according to which knowledge is an innate possession of reason) might spread across the border. So the government took some proactive steps to put down any dissent. On July 9, 1788, it issued the "Edict Concerning Religion," a clear attack on Enlightenment ideas that specifically enforced religious orthodoxy in churches. Friedrich hoped the edict would "repress, as much as possible, infidelity and superstition and by this means also the corruption of the fundamental truths of the Christian religion."[3]

More relevant for Kant was the "Edict of Censorship" that followed in December of the same year.[4] Free speech was central to Kant's political values. While he may have feared for his university position after the censorship edict, he still sought to defend freedom of expression and thought. In particular, he believed that any attempt to politically enforce religious orthodoxy could only damage the moral and political health of a nation. Thus, while the systematic drive behind *Religion* certainly relates it to Kant's previous writings, external political pressures played a major role in pushing Kant to set his thoughts to paper. The work's content clearly relates to the policies of the Prussian government.

NOTES

1   Immanuel Kant, *Critique of Practical Reason, Critique of Pure Reason, Critique on the Power of Judgment.*

2   Immanuel Kant, *Religion within the Boundaries of Mere Reason*, trans. and ed. Allen Wood and George Di Giovanni (Cambridge: Cambridge University Press, 1998), 37.

3   Guy Stanton Ford, "Wöllner and the Prussian Religious Edict of 1788," *The American Historical Review* 15, no. 3 (1910): 509.

4   See: Manfred Kuehn, *Kant: A Biography* (Cambridge: Cambridge University Press, 2001), 338ff.

MODULE 2
ACADEMIC CONTEXT

KEY POINTS

- In earlier works, Kant had argued that certain things were unknowable, including proof of the existence of God.

- While eighteenth-century philosophers explored many different ideas, rationalism* dominated within the university system.

- Kant was influenced by rationalism. He had already pointed out that while pure reason was an excellent way of understanding the world around us, there are things reason could not understand.

The Work in its Context

Immanuel Kant's *Religion within the Boundaries of Mere Reason* largely works within the intellectual parameters Kant set in the "critical" moral and theoretical philosophy he had developed over the previous two decades. Kant's three great *Critiques**[1] transformed the intellectual environment of Germany by presenting a revolutionary new orientation in philosophy based on two relatively simple premises.

First, Kant argued that the human faculty of reason had the capacity to investigate itself methodically; second, he argued that in so doing, it could establish both the scope and legitimacy of its own basic principles.

In other words, our minds can distinguish between what is knowable and what is essentially unknowable.

These principles helped establish what Kant saw as universal laws, which dictate how our minds experience nature and how we ought to act in relation to other rational subjects (that is, other

> ❝ The human being is justified, as rational, in testing all claims, all doctrines which impose respect upon him, before he submits to them. ❞
>
> Immanuel Kant, *Religion and Rational Theology*

individuals capable of rational action and reflection). Before writing *Religion*, Kant had found limits to theological* ideas of God and the soul; these things, he believed, were simply unknowable. This led to the logical conclusion that religion can be understood only with a pure practical faith based on *reason*. *Religion* was Kant's attempt to explain these theological reflections.

While eighteenth-century Germany entertained a variety of philosophical trends, the dominant school within university philosophy was the rationalism of the highly regarded philosophers Gottfried Leibniz* and Christian Wolff.* Kant's philosophy contested many of the central tenets of Leibnizian-Wolffian* rationalism, including its somewhat dogmatic theology. Rationalism relied on reason as the sole source of knowledge. This placed it in opposition to Kant's metaphysical* approach, which considered things, such as the world and God, that he believed transcended the limits of human experience; indeed, after Kant, rationalism declined in popularity.

Overview of the Field

By the time he wrote *Religion*, Kant had produced the major works of his "critical" philosophy; although German rationalist philosophers continued to fight Kant's influence, these *Critiques* had begun to find supporters who disseminated them within Germany. In effect, Kant founded his own school of thought—but no work remains free from external influences, and in the case of *Religion,* Kant evidently leverages the history of Christian doctrine. Critics still debate the level of the book's commitment to doctrine and the Christian theological tradition from which Kant primarily drew. Scholars generally agree that Lutheranism*—the branch of Protestant* Christianity in which Kant was raised—provides the theological backdrop for *Religion*.

By the eighteenth century, the principal theories underpinning rationalism had been most clearly defined by Wolff, who modified the works of Leibniz to make them more accessible. Leibniz's approach had been deterministic*—that is to say, he argued in favor of cause and effect. Leibniz also took the optimistic approach that although the universe is not perfect, it is nevertheless the best possible universe that God could have made.

Wolff supported both of these notions, but deviated from Leibniz in one key area.

Leibniz had argued that there existed in nature things he called "monads," which can be thought of as fundamental particles with clearly defined parameters. Monads came in all shapes and sizes—indeed, Leibniz believed that human beings were monads. Leibniz saw monads as unchanging, not subject to external laws of physics, and incapable of interacting with one another. Most importantly, Leibniz argued that these monads knew what to do and had in fact been pre-programmed with a unique set of instructions. Perhaps because of the obvious questions this raised relating to free will, Wolff shied away from the monad, reducing them to being "merely" an analogue of the soul, or else objects that could exist only on the atomic level.

Academic Influences

Through a modification of existing arguments, Kant's ideas stood in opposition to the traditional arguments of the rationalists.

The seventeenth-century French philosopher René Descartes* had helped establish the notion of reason as the chief source of all knowledge. While Descartes had conceded that aspects such as the discipline of physics could be understood only by means of real-life experience, he held that most knowledge, including epistemology* (the study of the nature of knowledge and belief) could be arrived at through reason alone. These ideas had been expanded over time by the seventeenth-century Dutch philosopher Benedictus Spinoza,* who introduced a system of logical ideas that built upon one another.

To understand the great leap of logic that Kant engineered, we must turn to the ideas of Leibniz and Wolff. Kant's innovation was to form his own set of ideas based upon a criticism of the rationalist school of thought, particularly the Leibnizian-Wolffian school. For Kant, philosophers had to explore the limits of reason. For this exploration, it would not do to reduce the monad to an esoteric concept such as the soul. The soul lay outside the mind's capacity for understanding. In the same way, we could never prove that we are living in the best possible universe. Kant named his ideas relating to the limits of reason "transcendental idealism." This concept would be reconceptualized in later years as the "absolute idealism"* of the late eighteenth- and early nineteenth-century German philosophers Friedrich Wilhelm Joseph von Schelling,* Johann Gottlieb Fichte,* and G. W. F. Hegel.*

NOTES

1 Immanuel Kant, *Critique of Practical Reason, Critique of Pure Reason, Critique on the Power of Judgment.*

MODULE 3
THE PROBLEM

KEY POINTS

- Kant's earlier philosophy maintained that some things such as the existence of God were impossible to prove.

- Traditional Christian theology argued that the Bible was the source of all moral authority and adherents must accept this notion based on faith.

- Kant felt that certain aspects, such as morality, could be understood by submitting them to critical reason.

Core Question

Immanuel Kant's *Religion within the Boundaries of Mere Reason* covers a number of themes in theology,* philosophy of religion,* ethics* (inquiry into morality and notions of "good" and "bad" actions) and metaphysics* (inquiry into the nature of being). While that may seem to encompass a wide range of disciplines, it is possible to unify them into a single question. And to do this, one must first look back at some of Kant's earlier work, particularly his *Critique of Pure Reason* (1781).[1]

Critique of Pure Reason details three core questions that Kant believed were fundamental: What can I know? What ought I to do? And what may I hope? He explored the first two questions fully in *Critique*; we may read *Religion* as an attempt to finish investigating the third. Why did he not answer the question in the same work in which he posed it? The answer has to do with Kant's belief that the domain of hope is occupied largely by religious and theological matters.

Kant's earlier work on critical philosophy had made it clear that the traditional doctrines of religion, especially those concerning God and the soul, were not theoretically provable. But because of

> **❝** So far as morality is based on the conception of the human being as one who is free but who also, just because of that, binds himself through his reason to unconditional laws, it is in need neither of the idea of another being above him in order that he recognize his duty, nor, that he observe it, of an incentive other than the law itself. **❞**
>
> Immanuel Kant, *Religion within the Boundaries of Mere Reason*

their supposedly necessary role within our moral thought, Kant exempted religious truths from the requirement of proof. Because they were so profound, Kant conceded that they might still permissibly be objects of hope. In other words, Kant argued that even though we could not *prove* that there is an afterlife, there may be reasonable justification to hope that there is one. In *Religion*, then, Kant attempts to provide a philosophically permissible account of religious truths that can and should serve as such objects of hope.

The Participants

Kant wrote *Religion* at a time of significant intellectual and political battles, which clearly shaped the work. He saw himself as a champion of the Enlightenment* and that intellectual movement's rational values, challenging the political and religious authorities of his day. *Religion* carries out that challenge by submitting religious belief and biblical theology to the tribunal of reason.

Kant makes a strong case for freedom of expression and of religious belief. Not surprisingly, the government's central censor in Berlin disliked the work. The censor could not ban it, however, because Kant had published it through his university's philosophy department. In doing that, Kant made a powerful statement against the government of King Friedrich Wilhelm II.* Many of the king's ministers, most prominently the politician and pastor Johann Christoph von Wöllner,* belonged to the reactionary religious order of the Rosicrucians.* Kant's moral and political outlook stood in stark opposition to their beliefs. In publishing *Religion*, Kant placed himself in the German Enlightenment tradition of the German Jewish philosopher Moses Mendelssohn's* *Jerusalem* (1783)[2] and the philosopher and critic Gotthold Ephraim Lessing's* *Education of the Human Race* (1780).[3]

Toward the end of the eighteenth century, religion and politics became intertwined. The authorities often treated attacks on religion in much the same way as an attack on the state itself. Earlier Enlightenment figures such as the seventeenth-century English philosopher Thomas Hobbes* had faced imprisonment for some of their ideas. Although that was less likely to happen to Kant, he certainly risked losing his university position.

As the Enlightenment progressed, it began to encroach upon areas that had been the province of the Church for a millennium. As far back as the early seventeenth century—more than a century before Kant wrote *Religion*—the English political theorist Robert Filmer* attempted to stem the tide of secular intervention into theological matters. Such arguments revolved around the sanctity of scripture* and the importance of faith in our understanding of God. Kant did not find either of those arguments satisfactory, but he agreed with their ultimate goal.

The Contemporary Debate

In Germany, the Enlightenment attitude to religion was considerably friendlier than it was in France or Britain. Writers such as François-Marie Arouet, who wrote under the pen name Voltaire,* and the Scottish philosopher David Hume* were hostile to Christian belief and doctrine. In fact, they openly mocked it. Kant's *Religion* reflects the more complex German approach—which is to say it is the product of received ideas. For example, unlike the majority of Kant's previous works, *Religion* explicitly takes up concepts and doctrines from the history of Christian theology. These include providence* (the care and guidance offered by God), grace* (God's unlimited capacity for forgiveness and blessings), and original sin* (the Christian doctrine that attributes the sinful nature of humanity to Adam and Eve's disobedience in the Garden of Eden).

That is not to say that Kant accepts the traditional theological explanations of these concepts. Indeed, he subjects them to significant modifications. He places them within the context of his own moral philosophy,* especially as presented in his *Critique of Practical Reason* (1788).[4] This is of course consistent with Kant's critical philosophy, which bases all morality on a single law of pure reason—that is, for Kant, we must base religious arguments about morality on pure reason alone. Only if these arguments drifted into areas Kant marked as unknowable could reason stop being the final arbiter of truth.

Scholars continue to debate the extent to which Kant actually relies upon traditional religious doctrines. Some have suggested that he may even use them to plug gaps and repair contradictions within his moral philosophy. He complicates the issue by frequently using biblical language and narrative at crucial points in a text that is nominally not about religion.

Kant's critical philosophy unquestionably challenged theology's supremacy as a moral authority. But *Religion* has a peculiarly ambiguous relation *to* religion. Kant's followers and others who have used the text in their own attempts to explore the nature and legitimacy of religion continue to reflect this ambiguity. Since *Religion* appeared relatively late in Kant's life, we must look to post-Kantian thought to understand how such ideas transformed schools such as the absolute idealism* of late-Enlightenment philosopher G. W. F. Hegel* and his near-contemporaries, Johann Gottlieb Fichte,* and Friedrich Wilhelm Joseph von Schelling,* as well as the Romantics*⁵—followers of a movement in thought, art, and literature that emphasized emotion as the source of aesthetics.

NOTES

1 Immanuel Kant, Critique of Pure Reason, trans. Paul Guyer and Allen Wood (Cambridge: Cambridge University Press, 1999).

2 Moses Mendelssohn, *Jerusalem: Or on Religious Power and Judaism*, trans. Allan Arkush (Massachusetts: Brandeis University Press, 1983).

3 Gotthold Ephraim Lessing, "The Education of the Human Race," in *Literary and Philosophical Essays*, ed. Charles W. Eliot (New York: P. F. Collier & Son, 1909–14).

4 Immanuel Kant, *Critique of Practical Reason*, trans. Mary McGregor (Cambridge: Cambridge University Press, 1997).

5 Paulo Diego Bubbio and Paul Redding, *Religion after Kant: God and Culture in the Idealist Era* (Newcastle: Cambridge Scholars Publishing, 2012), xiii.

THE AUTHOR'S CONTRIBUTION

KEY POINTS

- Kant wanted to challenge religious orthodoxy by demonstrating that one could know only so much about the nature of God.

- Philosophy and theology* (the systematic study of religious ideas) had long been considered separate disciplines. Kant brought the two fields closer together by asking philosophical questions about things that had traditionally been the sole province of religion.

- Kant had clearly been building toward these ideas for some time. *Religion* represents an application of his earlier critical theories to the sphere of theological thought.

Author's Aims

In writing *Religion within the Boundaries of Mere Reason*, Immanuel Kant was guided both by philosophical and religious concerns and by political considerations. He argued not only for religious freedom but for political freedom in general. The argument that "people" were not yet "ripe for freedom of belief,"[1] was in his view self-defeating, since freedom could not take hold until it had been established in reality.

However, Kant did add a caveat, stating that "given the circumstances of the time," he was not "in principle against the temporary curtailment of freedoms." Despite such backtracking, Kant opposed the idea that those whose freedom was temporarily taken away should then be treated as if they were "essentially not suited to freedom, and that one is justified in keeping them from it for all time." For Kant, such an act constituted an "intrusion into

> ❝ Now to unite the foundation of a moral faith (be this faith an end or merely an auxiliary means) with such an empirical faith which, to all appearances, chance has dealt to us, we require an interpretation of the revelation we happen to have, i.e. a thoroughgoing understanding of it in a sense that harmonizes with the universal practical rules of a pure religion of reason. ❞
>
> Immanuel Kant, *Religion within the Bounds of Mere Reason*

the prerogatives of Divinity itself, which created human beings for freedom."[2]

More explicitly, Kant intended *Religion* to legitimize religious commitments by founding them on a morality based upon reason, rather than religious or political authority. This notion was not particularly radical. Thinkers as far back as the seventeenth-century French philosopher René Descartes* had advocated the supremacy of reason. Kant's innovation was to apply his critical and systematic methodology to this question. In this sense he was successful, and his ideas remain influential.

Approach

In introducing the concept of radical evil, Kant sought to explain two things: first, which elements of religion people could understand by reason alone; and second, why any attempt to silence discussion of religion would be self-defeating.

In Kant's view, the evil nature of human beings connected to theological concepts such as original sin* (the Christian doctrine that humanity's inherently sinful nature results from the behavior of Adam and Eve in the Garden of Eden). He saw much of religious orthodoxy as centered on the journey to become a virtuous moral agent and so qualify for entry into heaven.*

In Parts I and II of *Religion*, Kant attempts to legitimize and interpret the doctrines of key Christian ideas such as original sin, divine grace* (God's unlimited benevolence), and redemption* (the Christian doctrine of forgiveness for sin) from a philosophical (rather than theological) viewpoint. Parts III and IV address the Church and religious practices more explicitly. In these, Kant outlines which institutions are compatible with a pure, rational faith. Part III offers an interpretation of the idea of the foundation of the Kingdom of God*—heaven—on earth and of divine providence. Kant explains how a community of believers basing their practice on "moral faith" alone should transcend a faith bounded by the structures of concrete ecclesiastical authorities and institutions. In Part IV he attacks the priesthood and a variety of religious practices more explicitly. Here, Kant dismisses much of religious practice as superstition or what he calls "counterfeit service." He contends that rather than being signifiers of faith they are instead obstacles to true moral faith.

Kant never denies God, however, attacking instead the Church's claim to somehow understand God; in doing so, he also questioned the Church's legitimacy and authority. Having established that many of the Church's practices lack legitimacy, Kant arrived at a single conclusion: the human species in its infancy was "a clever child and knew how to combine learning too, and even a philosophy helpful to the Church with propositions imposed upon him without any of his doing. But when he becomes a man, he puts away such childish things."[3] In short, society had matured beyond the need for God as an omnipresent arbiter of human morality.

Contribution in Context

Kant's work has profoundly influenced contemporary thought. Long before writing *Religion*, Kant had been exploring religious themes. Indeed, all three of the great *Critiques*[*4] that form the core of his mature "critical" philosophy dealt extensively with theological matters.

Although the *Critiques* sometimes expressed a more positive view of theology than *Religion*, there is one negative to be found in them. In fact, it may be the most important facet of Kant's contribution to the world of theological thought: the lengthy destruction of rational theology in the "Transcendental Dialectic"* section of the *Critique of Pure Reason* in which Kant attempts to describe what he terms the "dialectical" nature of pure human reason—how it falls into contradictions of its own making when it attempts to transcend experience and form concepts of the soul, God, and the cosmos.

Other works from Kant's critical period also suggest the themes and approaches of *Religion*. The 1786 essay "What Does It Mean to Orient Oneself in Thinking?" was Kant's contribution to the so-called "Pantheism controversy"* that shook German intellectual life in the mid-1780s.[5] In the essay, Kant set out his idea that theoretical knowledge was necessarily limited. The only theologically legitimate faith was pure practical faith based on the requirements of moral reasoning. Likewise, the "philosophical" reading of the beginning of Genesis, the first book of the Old Testament, in the short essay "Conjectural Beginning of Human History"[6] (also published in 1786), anticipated Kant's approach to religious scripture in *Religion*. He intended to promote an interpretation of the biblical passage using the guidelines of a pure, rational faith. But even before he wrote these two texts, Kant had clearly given some thought to the role of reason in his understanding of theology. For example, his 1784 essay "Idea for a Universal History with a Cosmopolitan Aim" anticipated the subject matter of *Religion*. In that essay, Kant attempted to justify an interpretation of human history as heading toward the establishment of an "ethical commonwealth."[7]

Of course, Kant's thoughts about morality and religion did not operate within a historical vacuum. But his work was so original and its impact has been so great that it generated a "school" of its own. To this day, scholars continue to label certain approaches to moral and religious themes "Kantian."

NOTES

1   Immanuel Kant, *Religion within the Boundaries of Mere Reason*, trans. and ed. Allen Wood and George Di Giovanni (Cambridge: Cambridge University Press, 1998), 180.

2   Kant, *Religion*, 180–1.

3   Kant, *Religion*, 127.

4   Immanuel Kant, *Critique of Practical Reason, Critique of Pure Reason, Critique on the Power of Judgment.*

5   Immanuel Kant, "What Does It Mean to Orient Oneself in Thinking?" in *Religion and Rational Theology*, ed. and trans. Allen Wood and George Di Giovanni (Cambridge: Cambridge University Press, 1996), 1–18.

6   Immanuel Kant, "Conjectural Beginning of Human History," in *Anthropology, History, and Education*, ed. Robert Louden and Günter Zöller (Cambridge: Cambridge University Press, 2011), 160–75.

7   Immanuel Kant, "Idea for a Universal History with a Cosmopolitan Aim," in *Anthropology*, ed. Louden and Zöller (Cambridge: Cambridge University Press, 2011), 107–20.

SECTION 2
IDEAS

MAIN IDEAS

KEY POINTS

- The three main themes of the text are man's propensity for grace,* good, and evil.

- Kant argued that because God was unknowable, humanity was responsible for its own moral choices.

- These ideas were presented as the third in a series of four questions. Kant did not address his fourth great question— "What is humanity?"— in *Religion.*

Key Themes

In *Religion within the Boundaries of Mere Reason*, Immanuel Kant developed several themes governing his examination of moral philosophy.* He looked at man's propensity for evil and for good and reworked the Christian concept of grace.

Philosophically, the work revolves around the possibility of what Kant calls the "highest good." Kant believed that practical reason could lead humanity to a more virtuous world in which people would not only maximize their virtue but could also achieve a level of happiness in proportion to their virtue.[1] As in his previous critical works, in *Religion* Kant aimed to articulate the rational theological framework we need to make sense of our moral predicament and possibly attain virtue.

Still, the world contains moral despair. The first two parts of *Religion* try to account for this by introducing two other important themes. First, Kant details his concept of the "propensity" for "radical evil" in human nature. Second, he explains how radical evil is forced to compete with a "good" principle.[2] It is not difficult

> ❝ All our knowledge begins with the senses, proceeds then to the understanding, and ends with reason. There is nothing higher than reason. ❞
>
> Immanuel Kant, *Critique of Pure Reason*

for human beings to navigate the path between radical evil and a "good disposition." So Kant detailed some ways in which people might follow the "good" path. Modifying the doctrine of grace was part of Kant's attempt to advise readers about a more proactive path to moral good. Yet he believed that path remained limited. For Kant, moral good still required God, regardless of how unknowable God might be.

Exploring the Ideas

Kant's discussion of the ideas of radical evil and moral conversion shapes the structure of Parts I and II of *Religion*. He derives both ideas from central doctrines in Christian theology. Radical evil is simply Kant's philosophical counterpart to original sin,* and moral conversion invokes the doctrines of redemption, grace, and atonement* (the reconciliation of God and sinful man through death and the resurrection of Jesus Christ).

Still, the relation between the traditional doctrines and Kant's interpretations remains complex and a continuing source of scholarly debate. Kant sees all human beings as having a propensity for radical evil. But while much Christian theology sees that evil as inherited, Kant thinks that people's moral failings create their evil dispositions. In attributing radical evil to human beings, Kant is relying on scripture,* but on a hypothesis gleaned empirically*— that is, from observable evidence (in this case human behavior and history). Kant sees evil as contrary to our nature.[3] Our maxims— the principles upon which we act—dictate right and wrong, and we seem to know the difference. Kant believed that human beings should use maxims to prioritize moral law over actions that merely meet our personal ends—but that people have a tendency to make exceptions for themselves; a married man with a mistress, for example, knows on some level that he is violating the maxim of fidelity.

From a psychological perspective, Kant believes that human self-love gives us a tendency to view our own actions as righteous. He also identified two further causes of moral despair: our inability to see whether we are contributing to worldly good or evil and our immoral habit of deceiving ourselves about the quality of our intentions.

Radical evil obviously has negative consequences. So human beings need moral conversion—a "revolution," as Kant says—to transform their dispositions from evil to good.[4] Crucially, Kant argued that people are just as responsible for creating this revolution as we are for our evil natures. To grasp this radical notion, one must first understand the concept of grace as Kant saw it.

In traditional theology, grace represents God's propensity to both love and forgive humanity. Kant, however, rejected this notion. To him, one should not expect to receive forgiveness after behaving in a morally reprehensible way. Rather, he thought, we should avoid needing forgiveness by acting in a moral way in the first place. In Kant's reading of the Bible, even Jesus Christ— the son of God—advocated that human beings should avoid sin rather than seek forgiveness for it. Scholars remain puzzled about whether Kant was appealing to specific theological doctrines with this discussion, and if so, to which. He seems to imply that we require grace, especially "justificatory grace" that "imputes" righteousness to us. In Kant's view, any moral conversion must be entirely a matter of our own effort.[5]

Language and Expression

It is not easy to determine what within this combination of themes matters most to Kant. Yet it is important to note the function *Religion* played within Kant's overall critical philosophy. In a letter of May 1793 to a theology professor at the University of Göttingen called K. F. Stäudlin,* Kant reprised a list of questions he wrote near the end of his *Critique of Pure Reason* over a decade earlier. Kant identified these questions as being of essential interest to human reason. In the letter he presents them as providing the orientation for his entire philosophy.

"The plan that I made for myself some time ago as I prepared to work in the field of pure philosophy called for the resolution of three problems: 1) What can I know? (Metaphysics); 2) What ought I to do? (Morality); 3) What may I hope for? (Religion)."[6]

By categorizing the questions into those of metaphysics, morality, and religion, Kant offers some insight into *Religion*: It is a vehicle through which Kant can return to and explore questions he raised earlier. The work assumes the reader's familiarity with his earlier books and the novel terminology he introduced in them, in which words such as "transcendental" and "reason" have been put to very specific ends. Kant goes further in *Religion* than he did in the letter or in his earlier *Critique*,* adding a fourth great question: "What is humankind?"

Unfortunately, he does not answer this essential question. So *Religion* is in a sense only the middle section of a much larger text. Readers who tackle only this one work potentially miss both the beginning and the end of the story.

The biblical and theological language in *Religion* poses an additional difficulty. Kant clearly states in the preface that the Bible's content must be presented and justified according to moral reason. Although, his extensive use of biblical language, especially from John's Gospel (an account of Jesus Christ and his teaching from the New Testament*) and the letters of St. Paul (New Testament texts considered foundational for Christian theology), often blurs the boundaries between theology and his own moral philosophy.

NOTES

1   Immanuel Kant, *Critique of Practical Reason* (Cambridge: Cambridge University Press, 1997), 5: 124ff.

2   Immanuel Kant, *Religion within the Boundaries of Mere Reason*, trans. and ed. Allen Wood and George Di Giovanni (Cambridge: Cambridge University Press, 1998), parts I and II.

3   Kant, *Religion*, 59.

4   Kant, *Religion*, xviii.

5   Kant, *Religion*, xxiii.

6   Immanuel Kant, *Correspondence*, trans. and ed. Arnulf Zweig (Cambridge: Cambridge University Press, 1999), 458.

MODULE 6
SECONDARY IDEAS

KEY POINTS

- *Religion* offers two secondary ideas: the founding of the Kingdom of God—that is, heaven*—and the idea of "counterfeit service."*

- By articulating these controversial ideas, Kant merely reflected the moods of the time.

- Removing the Church's monopoly on matters of morality would have a profound influence on the course of human history.

Other Ideas

Parts III and IV of Immanuel Kant's *Religion within the Boundaries of Mere Reason* contain the work's secondary themes. These include the founding of the Kingdom of God*—usually understood to be heaven—and the idea of counterfeit service (that is, signifiers of faith that serve as obstacles to true moral faith). The rituals and the historical role of the Church take center stage in these sections.

In Part III, "Concerning the victory of the good over the evil principle and the founding of a Kingdom of God on earth," Kant contrasts "ecclesiastical faith" (the faith practiced and taught by the Church) with "moral faith." He contends that the latter alone will be present in the true "ethical commonwealth"* or the "Kingdom of God."

Kant then advocates lessening the role of the Church in matters of morality. In the commonwealth he describes, moral agents (individuals capable of acting morally) form a community bound by moral laws alone. According to Kant, God establishes these laws;

> **❝** But to unite in a permanent religious institution which is not to be subject to doubt before the public even in the lifetime of one man, and thereby to make a period of time fruitless in the progress of mankind toward improvement, thus working to the disadvantage of posterity—that is absolutely forbidden. For himself (and only for a short time) a man may postpone enlightenment in what he ought to know, but to renounce it for posterity is to injure and trample on the rights of mankind. **❞**
>
> Immanuel Kant, "An Answer to the Question: What Is Enlightenment?"

they are not enforced by any political or Church authority. Kant invokes the theological notion of providence* (divine care and intervention in the course of human history), contending that the Kingdom of God is an object of hope. We may see history as a gradual progression toward the realization of this ethical commonwealth. It should be noted, also, that Kant was writing in the context of the Enlightenment,* an intellectual project that aimed to advance the condition of humanity through the exercise of rational behavior and ideals.

In Part IV, "Concerning service and counterfeit service under the dominion of the good principle, or, of religion and priestcraft," Kant also concerns himself with the progressive historical transition to an ethical commonwealth. Here, he identifies the practices and rituals of "historical religion" as contingent historical products and, therefore, not essential for true moral faith.

Exploring the Ideas

Kant's understanding of the Kingdom of God as a political or religious body continues to provoke scholarly debate. On the one hand, the themes of Part III resonate with his political writings, such as "Perpetual Peace," a work that describes how conflict and competition will gradually establish a peaceful order of states with republican constitutions.[1] This might imply that, for Kant, the Kingdom of God is a worldly affair—an idea that contrasts with the orthodox Church view that the Kingdom of God can be found only in heaven. Since Kant used religious language to invoke traditional theological concepts and the Kingdom's status as an object of hope, some commentators argue that the Kingdom should have a more spiritual interpretation (or at least an interpretation more grounded in theology).

Kant's views on counterfeit service tie in quite strongly with his belief that certain things—the afterlife, for example—remain essentially unknowable. At best, Kant regards the rituals of the Church as *provisional* vehicles for genuine morality. Over time, these rituals gradually become more rational and should eventually be abandoned as a properly "natural religion" develops, based on moral laws alone.[2]

Kant is not content, however, with merely assigning a historical role to the Church. He also thinks the Church has damaged true faith, observing: "How quickly these blind and external professions ... can if they yield means of gain, bring about a certain falsehood in a community's very way of thinking."[3]

In particular, he condemns such practices as prayer and pilgrimage. Having little to do with promoting moral action, Kant sees them merely as a way to placate and win favor with God. Moreover, once we invest historically contingent rituals—that is, rituals that function only in a certain historical context—with religious and moral importance, the priesthood can wield dangerous power and become debilitated by hypocrisy. We should note, however, that in Part IV Kant does not simply direct gratuitous abuse at religious institutions. He intends this portion of *Religion* especially to have real-world applications and offers, in part, a commentary on his own times. In particular, Part IV contains barely concealed political arguments for domestic freedom of religion and expression.

Overlooked

Over the course of more than two centuries, thousands of scholarly books and articles have been written on the major areas of Kant's thought. His ideas on religion are no exception. Kant played an important role in the emergence of the philosophy of religion* as an independent subject and in the decline of the intellectual authority of theology as a discipline. Even so, *Religion* has received less attention than his *Critiques*,*[4] especially in the twentieth century.

Instead, twentieth-century scholars examined Kant as an epistemologist*—someone who inquires into the nature of knowledge. These scholars focused on Kant's famous division of appearances and "things-in-themselves" set forth in his *Critiques*. In the twenty-first century, philosophers of religion have renewed their examination of *Religion*. This shift stems in part from a recent tendency to argue that Kant's work has relevance to metaphysics* (the philosophical study of the ultimate nature of reality or being). Kant, though, would likely disagree with this tendency.

However, if one views Kant's entire philosophical project, it shows sensitivity to the spiritual dimensions of our lives, especially our moral and aesthetic experiences. Scholars have demonstrated how Kant's mature critical project links with his earlier philosophy, which frequently dealt with explicitly theological concerns.[5]

A further area of research around *Religion* concerns the specific theological and confessional sources of the doctrines it alludes to or directly discusses. Kant's discussion of grace* is one example of this. Despite his childhood Pietism*—an offshoot of the Protestant* branch of the Christian faith that stressed personal piety, religious experience, and the role of conscience in the religious life—Kant's thinking on this theme has resonances with traditions we might associate with the Catholic branch of Christianity before the Reformation* (the events of the sixteenth century that led to the formation of the Protestant church).[6]

Investigating both the specific doctrinal ideas that influenced Kant and the histories of those ideas may offer clues that help scholars interpret the more obscure passages of this frequently perplexing text.

NOTES

1   Immanuel Kant, "Perpetual Peace" (New York: Cosimo, 2005), 3–28.

2   Immanuel Kant, *Religion within the Boundaries of Mere Reason*, trans. and ed. Allen Wood and George Di Giovanni (Cambridge: Cambridge University Press, 1998), 169.

3   Kant, *Religion*, 28.

4   Immanuel Kant, *Critique of Practical Reason, Critique of Pure Reason, Critique on the Power of Judgment.*

5   See: Christopher J. Insole, *Kant and the Creation of Freedom: A Theological Problem* (Oxford: Oxford University Press, 2013).

6   See: Jacqueline Mariña, "Kant on Grace: A Reply to His Critics," *Religious Studies* 33 (1997): 379–400.

ACHIEVEMENT

KEY POINTS

- Kant envisioned a religion less dominated by the doctrines of the Church. This eventually found limited expression in the twentieth century, as liberal democracies—governments founded on notions of individual liberty, in which elections are regularly held—became more secular.

- Kant championed reason over superstition. This forms an important part of an ongoing narrative of philosophical achievements that has helped humanity create today's modern world.

- Kant was unable to criticize political and theological ideas directly due to the risk of legal censure.

Assessing the Argument

Immanuel Kant's *Religion within the Boundaries of Mere Reason* was guided as much by political intentions as by religious concerns. In evaluating the work, we must therefore consider both aspects. His challenge to King Friedrich Wilhelm II's* religious orthodoxy reflected the specific circumstances of the time. Kant avoided the theological censor by publishing *Religion* as a philosophical text. And as the ideas espoused by Kant and his peers in the Enlightenment* took root, both religious and political censorship declined and liberal democracies grew.

Kant had a somewhat prophetic view of the relation between reason and theology. This is especially clear in *Religion*. Six decades after the work, the English naturalist Charles Darwin* established

> ❝ Out of the crooked timber of humanity, no
> straight thing was ever made. ❞
>
> Immanuel Kant, "Idea for a Universal History with a Cosmopolitan Aim"

the field of evolutionary biology* with his revolutionary work
On the Origin of the Species. Interpreting the Bible less literally also
became more acceptable. Of course, Kant had already floated the
idea that central concepts of religion are not objects of theoretical
knowledge. Scholars frequently present this as having dealt a blow
to religion and theology. Yet Kant clearly wanted to find a place for
religion within his thought.

In tying religious doctrines to the phenomena of hope, moral
despair, freedom, and natural beauty, Kant opened avenues for his
critique to be applied to theological metaphysics—inquiries into
the nature of being that draw on the aims and methods of theology.
The German philosopher Friedrich Schleiermacher,* for example,
one of the founders of liberal theology, was deeply influenced by
Kant, although he understood religion to be based on one's feeling
of dependence on God rather than on theoretical proofs. Later in
the nineteenth century, the Danish philosopher Søren Kierkegaard*
would locate religious phenomena and value in areas of human
life that transcended aesthetic* experience (the sensual experiences
of facets such as beauty and art) and everyday moral and political
experience. Like Schleiermacher before him, Kierkegaard did not
found his arguments on theoretical proofs.

Achievement in Context

As we have seen, in *Religion*, Kant builds on ideas he had already
expressed in earlier works. To a certain extent, the world was not yet
ready for some of the ideas in *Religion*. With hindsight, it is relatively
easy to see that the rise of Enlightenment thought correlated

with the declining influence of theology. But Kant could not have known that this would happen. Still, he argued in favor of replacing traditional religion with one based on pure, practical faith—even if he offered no timeframe for this transition.

It is true, however, that *Religion*, together with Kant's broader thinking on faith, played a crucial role in the emergence of the philosophy of religion* as a distinct philosophical enterprise.

The most significant German philosopher before Kant, Gottfried Wilhelm von Leibniz,* wished not only to mediate between modern philosophy and theology but also to unite the thought of the two principle branches of Christianity: Protestantism and Catholicism. In his *Critique of Pure Reason* (1781),[1] Kant argued that the kinds of theological knowledge at the heart of Leibniz's system were not even possible. In his moral and religious writings, Kant seeks to provide new, non-theoretical grounds for religious belief. He finds them in the moral life and in aesthetic experience. The effects of these changes can already be seen in the work of the most famous post-Kantian philosopher, G. W. F. Hegel,* who was about 50 years younger than Kant. Hegel would lecture on the "philosophy of religion," a topic that had a definite place within his overall system. Kant was able to bridge the gaps between the centuries by providing a method to gradually reduce the role of the Church in society.

Limitations

After the publication of *Religion*, the Prussian pastor and politician Johann Christoph von Wöllner* wrote to Kant at the king's behest. He charged Kant with defaming Christianity and thereby failing in his duties as an educator of Prussian youth. Kant replied: "I am not guilty of disparaging Christianity in that book, since it contains no assessment of any actual revealed religion. It is intended merely as an examination of rational religion."[2] That is to say, his book did not inquire into Christianity in particular, but only those religious ideas which Kant felt related to a morality that could be based on pure practical reason. Such comments reveal a limitation: Kant did not see *Religion* as a comment on Christianity. Instead, he claimed his intent was universal in scope. Kant's ideas had little chance of resonating with the politically minded intellectuals of the time. No immediate political change would be forthcoming.

Although he thought he might be able to have an impact on theological matters, his idea of pure practical reason seemed, nevertheless, incompatible with Christianity. The German theologian Karl Friedrich Stäudlin* was quick to point this out in a 1793 letter to Kant:

"Conscientiousness and true respect for the Christian religion have been my guide in this work, but also the principle of a befitting candor: to conceal nothing but rather to lay open how I believe that I see a possible union of the Christian religion with the purest practical reason."[3]

While Kant's reply to Wöllner was politically motivated, he honestly did intend his work to present a purely universal religion of reason. He saw a rational faith as something that anyone may commit to as an autonomous moral agent. Even readers willing to argue for the universal character of Kant's major critical works, however, face a more difficult task when it comes to *Religion*. Many of the concepts it considers, such as God and providence* (the idea of God as intervening in events in order to direct human history), have their counterparts in a range of major religions. But Kant's particular versions of these doctrines remain distinctly Christian; for example, he discusses providence in the context of the founding of the Kingdom of God.* He also relies heavily upon New Testament* language and quotations to discuss distinctively Christian conceptions of grace* (God's limitless forgiveness) and atonement* (the process by which human beings can make good their sins and receive grace).

NOTES

1   Immanuel Kant, *Critique of Pure Reason*, trans. Paul Guyer and Allen Wood
    (Cambridge: Cambridge University Press, 1999).

2   Immanuel Kant, *Correspondence*, trans. and ed. Arnulf Zweig (Cambridge:
    Cambridge University Press, 1999), 487.

3   Kant, *Correspondence*, 458.

MODULE 8
PLACE IN THE AUTHOR'S WORK

KEY POINTS

- Kant's body of work examined the limits of reason and what we can truly know about reality.

- *Religion* continues Kant's exploration of the human condition. In effect it answers the question: What may we hope?

- By the time *Religion* was published, Kant had a well-established reputation as one of the greatest thinkers of all time. Delving into areas he only touched upon in other works, *Religion* remains an important, if distinct, area of study.

Positioning

After writing *Religion within the Boundaries of Mere Reason*, Immanuel Kant primarily produced short essays that do not appear to substantially alter or develop his previous positions. The exceptions are *The Metaphysics of Morals* (1797)[1] and the so-called *Opus Postumum*,[2] a collection of writings published as an edited volume in the 1930s. The latter is the somewhat repetitive and fragmentary manuscript Kant had been working on before he died. While scholars debate its importance to Kant's central critical philosophy, it does suggest that he came to think of God as something human beings can understand rationally. Earlier works, including *Religion*, retained traces of the idea of a transcendent God[3]—something beyond human experience or understanding.

Some of Kant's later essays such as "On the Old Saw: That May be Right in Theory, but It Won't Work in Practice" (1793)[4] and

> **❝Thoughts without content are empty, intuitions without concepts are blind.❞**
>
> Immanuel Kant, *Critique of Pure Reason*

"The End of All Things"[5] from 1794 resume theological themes. But these essays do not alter the doctrines of *Religion*, which was in many respects as much a work of political as of religious thought. Kant takes up some of *Religion*'s political motifs in later works such as *The Metaphysics of Morals* (1797) and the essays "Perpetual Peace" (1795)[6] and "The Conflict of the Faculties" (1798)[7]. The third part of *Religion* is particularly relevant to these later works, since it discusses the establishment of an ethical commonwealth* or Kingdom of God among moral agents—individuals capable of acting morally.

Such a place transcends any merely civic or political entity because it binds its people only by moral laws. While *The Metaphysics of Morals* develops the principles governing the formation and maintenance of a political order, "Perpetual Peace" and "The Conflict of the Faculties" take up the question of the relationship between the inner moral order of the ethical commonwealth and the external legal order of a political society. In the latter text, Kant shifts to the idea that establishing a political order of republics in peaceful coexistence is a precondition of an ethical commonwealth, rather than the reverse.

Integration

In *Religion*, Kant continues to engage with the three main questions that represent his life's work. The answer to the question "What may I hope?" is self-contained, though the process through which Kant arrived at the answer is not. The techniques and requirements of Kant's critical philosophy are still as present in *Religion* as they are in what is unquestionably his most important work, the *Critique of Pure Reason.* Indeed, *Religion* is linked with Kant's earlier work through a distinctively Kantian philosophical vocabulary that includes words and phrases such as *a priori** (a thought that is separate from experience). Kant's critical works form an intellectually unified corpus, with the three *Critiques**8 at their foundation. Kant intended his critical thought to be systematic. To properly understand the text, one must grasp at least one aspect of this systematic approach: Kant's philosophy follows a transcendental* method. He explores this methodology, summarized here, in earlier works.

According to the transcendental method, reason investigates itself to legitimize its conclusions and to discover its own limits.

One can imagine a search engine within a web browser. By inputting words, a user can receive information from a variety of sources. Though this is unquestionably a useful tool, one cannot assume the accuracy of the information. For instance, although we can ask certain questions such as "How old am I?" we can almost guarantee that the browser will provide unsatisfactory answers. The limitations of our search engine correlate with Kant's idea that reason has limits.

This also relates to Kant's foundational doctrine of rational autonomy*—the idea that rational beings control their own foundational principles for comprehending and acting within the world. In *Religion*, Kant's approach to theological doctrine is governed by his conviction that any doctrine must accord with the moral autonomy of human beings. In this sense, we should not view Kant's body of work as disjointed but, rather, as modular. Of course, Kant did adjust certain ideas over the course of his long life. And later thinkers such as G. W. F. Hegel* would also modify them to fit their own theories. But Kant's work—including *Religion*—remains remarkably consistent.

Significance

Kant wrote *Religion* late in his career. Most of the important texts of his "critical" philosophy had already been published, primarily in his three *Critiques*. *Religion* has been rather more neglected than his major critical works, especially in the twentieth century. But it addresses central themes of critical practical philosophy, particularly about the nature of the will. Scholars still debate whether *Religion* contains crucial developments of Kant's moral philosophy* or whether it simply applies pre-established conceptions to the field of theology.* The importance of this question depends upon one's attitude to theology.

Kant had a political motive for writing the text. But whatever his purpose, *Religion* remains a lesser text only in relation to the rest of Kant's remarkable body of work. His *Critique of Pure Reason* (1781) established Kant as one of the greatest thinkers of all time. This in effect dictated the direction of his life. And one cannot overstate its influence on later thinkers such as the idealist* philosophers Hegel, Friedrich Wilhelm Joseph von Schelling,* and Johann Gottlieb Fichte.*

Religion's principal criticisms of traditional church-based faith undoubtedly supported, if not directly contributed to, the rise of secularism, especially as it relates to formal political institutions. Critics often debated Kant's ideas during his lifetime; the extent of their influence is extraordinary.

NOTES

1   Immanuel Kant, *Groundwork of the Metaphysics of Morals*, in *Cambridge Texts in the History of* Philosophy (Cambridge: Cambridge University Press, 2012).

2   Immanuel Kant, *Opus Postumum* in *The Cambridge Edition of the Works of Immanual Kant,* eds. Eckart Förster and Michael Rosen (Cambridge: Cambridge University Press, 1995).

3   See: Christopher J. Insole, *Kant and the Creation of Freedom: A Theological Problem* (Oxford: Oxford University Press, 2013), 168ff.

4   Immanuel Kant, *On the Old Saw: That May be Right in Principle but it Won't Work in Practice,* trans. E. B. Ashton (Pennsylvania: University of Pennsylvania Press, 1974).

5   Immanuel Kant, *The End of All Things,* in *Religion within the Boundaries of Mere Reason and Other Writings*, ed. Allen Wood and George Di Giovanni (Cambridge: Cambridge University Press, 1998), 191–203.

6   Immanuel Kant, "Perpetual Peace" (New York: Cosimo, 2005).

7   Immanuel Kant, *The Conflict of the Faculties*, trans. Mary J. McGregor (Nebraska: University of Nebraska Press, 1992).

8   Immanuel Kant, *Critique of Practical Reason, Critique of Pure Reason, Critique on the Power of Judgment.*

SECTION 3
IMPACT

THE FIRST RESPONSES

KEY POINTS

- People objected to *Religion* for a variety of reasons. King Friedrich Wilhelm II* saw it as an attack on orthodox religion, while intellectuals saw it as a step backward for the great thinker Kant to write about scripture.*

- Kant promised the king he would not write or lecture on religion, so he did not immediately respond to criticism. When he did so, he argued against religious censorship.

- Political censorship was certainly the most important factor in the response to *Religion*. Kant was mostly silent about the work from its publication in 1793 until the king died in 1797.

Criticism

The first significant response to Immanuel Kant's *Religion within the Boundaries of Mere Reason* came from the political world. In October 1794, Johann Christoph von Wöllner,* a Prussian politician and pastor, wrote to Kant on behalf of the king:

"Our most high person has long observed with great displeasure how you misuse your philosophy to distort and negatively evaluate many of the cardinal and basic teachings of the Holy Scripture and of Christianity; how you have done this particularly in your book *Religion within the Boundaries of Mere Reason,* as well as in shorter treatises. We expected better things of you as you yourself must realize how irresponsibly you have acted against your duty as a teacher of the youth."[1]

Wöllner demanded that Kant explain himself. He also

> ❝ Our age is the age of criticism, to which everything must be subjected. The sacredness of religion, and the authority of legislation, are by many regarded as grounds of exemption from the examination of this tribunal. But, if they are exempted, they become the subjects of just suspicion, and cannot lay claim to sincere respect, which reason accords only to that which has stood the test of a free and public examination. ❞
>
> Immanuel Kant, *Critique of Pure Reason*

threatened Kant with "unpleasant measures"—such as losing his university position—should he continue to be obstinate. Both Wöllner and the king had transparent motives—not based on any substantial engagement with the text. They wanted to reverse the Enlightenment*-inspired rationalist* policies of Friedrich Wilhelm's father, Friedrich II* and they wanted to enforce religious orthodoxy both in the Church and in the academic world.

Religion had its critics at the other end of the interpretive spectrum as well. The work disappointed certain German intellectuals, including the poet and playwright Johann Wolfgang von Goethe,* who noted that in his previous works Kant had breathed the spirit of the Enlightenment. Kant had made reason the tribunal (that is, the judge) of authorities (including that of reason itself). But the man who had once championed the autonomy of the rational individual was now sullying himself with biblical interpretation and theological doctrine. In particular, Goethe found Kant's idea of radical evil too close to a traditional notion of original sin.* The twentieth-century German philosopher Ernst Cassirer* notes that Goethe had "remarked bitterly in a letter to [the German philosopher] Herder* that Kant has disgracefully 'slobbered on' his philosopher's cloak 'with the blot of radical evil, so that even Christ would be enticed to kiss its hem.'"[2]

Responses

The contemporary political response to the text may have been intellectually insignificant, but some scholars continue to interpret *Religion* as adversarial to religion. They note that it arguably wishes to replace religion with moral philosophy.* Cassirer, for example, offers a clear example of such an interpretation, writing that "the substance of his philosophy of religion comprises for [Kant] only a confirmation of and a corollary of the substance of his ethics. *Religion* 'within the limits of reason alone' ... has no essential content other than that of pure morality. The conversion of pure rational religion into pure ethics is required."[3]

If that had indeed been Kant's purpose, his response to such accusations made by his contemporaries verged on the disingenuous. He insisted that he was a responsible teacher who by no means disparaged religion in his lectures. Even so, he did give in to the king's demands, writing: "I believe the surest way, which will obviate the least suspicion, is for me to declare solemnly, as Your Majesty's loyal subject, that I will hereafter refrain altogether from discoursing publicly, in lectures or writings, on religion, whether natural or revealed."[4]

Kant's dispute with Wöllner (and, by proxy, with the king) occurred while he was an old man, and long after he had written the major works that secured his reputation. We cannot really say that he engaged in a critical dialogue about *Religion*. Nor did he revise its central arguments as a result of his promise to the king.

Kant waited until the king's death in 1797 to publish another text that engaged with the topic of religion: the essay "The Conflict of the Faculties."[5]

Conflict and Consensus

While Kant's agreement to neither lecture nor write about religion lasted only until the king's death, he did take up certain key themes of *Religion* in later essays. He particularly focused on the notions regarding the establishment of an ethical commonwealth* based on purely moral laws that he discusses in Part III. In his 1795 essay "Perpetual Peace,"[6] Kant describes this commonwealth as a community based on moral virtue that assures perpetual peace. He implies that establishing such a virtuous community under purely "divine" laws must precede the establishment of manmade laws to ensure peaceful relations between states.

In his essay "The Conflict of the Faculties," Kant also wrote about the circumstances surrounding the publication of *Religion*. He argued that philosophers should not have to submit their work to theology faculties for approval and that while philosophers ought to uphold biblical faith, they should submit that faith to the critique of reason. This text also argues that an external political order securing peace between nations must precede the establishment of communities of free beings who live in harmony by subjecting themselves to moral law and cultivating virtue. This directly contradicts his argument in "Perpetual Peace."

These later works once more pose the question of how Kant conceives the ethical commonwealth he called the "Kingdom of God"* in *Religion*. How does Kant conceive the relationship between human history and divine providence?* If humanity's destiny is to live in an ethical commonwealth, is this a transcendent condition (heaven itself), an impending historical and political reality, or an object of hope needed to orient and sustain us in our moral efforts?

The lack of external criticism of any real significance demonstrates Kant's status as one of the greatest thinkers of all time.

NOTES

1   Manfred Kuehn, *Kant: A Biography* (Cambridge: Cambridge University Press, 2001), 389.

2   Ernst Cassirer, *Kant's Life and Thought*, trans. James Haden (New Haven: Yale University Press, 1981), 391.

3   Cassirer, *Kant's Life*, 381.

4   Immanuel Kant, *Correspondence*, trans. and ed. Arnulf Zweig (Cambridge: Cambridge University Press, 1999), 486.

5   Immanuel Kant, *The Conflict of the Faculties*, trans. Mary J. McGregor (Nebraska: University of Nebraska Press, 1992).

6   Immanuel Kant, "Perpetual Peace" (New York: Cosimo, 2005).

THE EVOLVING DEBATE

KEY POINTS

- Kant's argument that philosophy should be kept separate from religious thought resonated and gained traction over the years. Today we consider the disciplines of theology and philosophy as entirely separate, touching only within the field of the philosophy of religion.*

- While no schools of thought arose from *Religion*, it did help establish the philosophy of religion as a separate academic field.

- The text had limited impact in its day, although the Catholic* Church suppressed its ideas for a time. Kant's religious ideas had more influence on Protestant* thinking.

Uses and Problems

Immanuel Kant's *Religion within the Boundaries of Mere Reason* transformed several intellectual fields and disciplines. He inherited a university system in Germany in which philosophy was intimately bound up with theological themes. Contemporary philosophy took its orientations from the theological tradition as typified by the then-dominant Leibnizian-Wolffian* school.

The seventeenth-century German philosopher Gottfried Wilhelm Leibniz* placed the metaphysical* concepts of God, the self, and the world at the heart of a systematically integrated philosophy. These were the very concepts Kant criticized as illusions in his *Critique of Pure Reason*. Leibniz attempted to reconcile the philosophy that arose following the scientific revolution with

> **66** That the whole form of the method is a triplicity, is merely the superficial external side of the mode of cognition; but to have demonstrated even this must also be regarded as an infinite merit of the Kantian philosophy. **99**
>
> G. W. F. Hegel, *The Science of Logic*

the philosophical theology of the medieval scholastic* tradition (a method of learning that emphasizes dialectical reasoning: the process of discovering contradictions by inferring truths from observations of new or prior thought).

He also made it his aim to navigate a harmonious path between Protestantism and Catholicism.

Kant saw human reason as an ultimate authority—a radical departure from consensus. While the eighteenth-century Scottish philosopher David Hume* also launched attacks on natural theology, his approach was self-consciously critical; Kant, rather, devoted considerable energy to providing derivations and justification of central religious concepts by making them products of pure practical reason. But he did not wish to replace religion—he wished only to modify its form. Indeed, according to Kant, religion "free from every dogma is inscribed in the heart of all human beings."[1]

Kant wanted to position philosophy not as an aid to theology based upon revelation, but as a way to explore the role religious concepts play within the economy of human reason. Kant's insistence that we should judge theological and religious doctrines according to morality rather than the converse was intimately related to this shift. He intended the doctrines discussed by *Religion* to flow from the human predicament of being a free, autonomous, but ultimately finite being.

Schools of Thought

Kant's philosophy of religion has had an enormous impact upon subsequent Protestant thought, among both orthodox and liberal (unorthodox) schools. The first significant post-Kantian theologian was the nineteenth-century German philosopher Friedrich Schleiermacher.* His attempt to base theology in a feeling of absolute dependence upon the divine would have been unthinkable without Kant's arguments.[2] Karl Barth,* one of the most significant opponents of Schleiermacher's liberal theology in the twentieth century, was similarly influenced by Kant's epistemology* (Kant's approach to inquiry into the nature of knowledge). Barth wrote that "pure ethics require—and here we are in complete agreement with Kant—that there should be no mixing of heaven and earth in the sphere of morals."[3]

Kant had a less pronounced influence on Catholic thought. The Vatican placed the Italian translation of the *Critique of Pure Reason*,[4] in which he attacks metaphysical speculation about God and the soul, on its Index of Prohibited Books in 1827. In the nineteenth century, the Catholic Church found Kantian thought incompatible with its attempt to revive Thomism*—the philosophy of the medieval theologian St. Thomas Aquinas.* Nevertheless, Karl Rahner,* one of the major Catholic theologians of the twentieth century, engaged deeply with Kant. Kant's methodology influenced his own and was vital to his explanation of the nature of religious experience and its relation to thought and morality.[5]

In his 1919 work *Religion of Reason out of the Sources of Judaism*, the German philosopher Hermann Cohen* attempted to synthesize Kant's philosophy of religion with Jewish ethics.[6] By assigning morality a theoretical priority in his discussion of religion, Cohen placed himself firmly in the Kantian tradition. He attempts to articulate a "religion of reason" while tying it to the basic concepts of Judaism. Such an endeavor is certainly ironic, given Kant's attitude to Judaism in *Religion*. He dismisses it as a historically redundant system of political laws that entails "absolutely no religious faith."[7]

Kant denied that the objects of religion are a matter of theoretical cognition. His legacy in this regard includes some of the most prominent historical attacks on religion. Thinkers such as the nineteenth-century German philosopher Ludwig Feuerbach,* who influenced the philosopher and revolutionary socialist Karl Marx,* explained religion in terms of psychological theories of projection. In the twentieth century, Sigmund Freud,* the founder of modern psychoanalysis, would follow suit.

In Current Scholarship

No philosopher today accepts any of Immanuel Kant's ideas wholesale. *Religion* cannot be said to have contemporary disciples. Although moral philosophers may look to the text for enlightenment on concepts that have a bearing on Kant's general moral philosophy,* *Religion*'s deep engagement with the Bible and Christian theology makes it largely incompatible with modern philosophy.

Nevertheless, as the philosophy of religion has grown as a discipline, several philosophers who have greater sympathy for religious themes have produced studies of the text. Contemporary American scholars Nathan Jacobs* and Chris Firestone*[8] provide an interpretation of the text marked by the idea that Kant is not some militant secularist or destroyer of traditional religion. They make the case that he bases his philosophy on a real commitment to central Christian doctrines such as the Incarnation (the word denoting the Christian belief that Jesus Christ was God incarnated—made flesh—on earth) and grace.* Kant's treatment of these themes, they argue, is not merely allegorical. He is not attempting to render religious terms in a purely moral philosophical way.

Very few scholars have adopted this affirmative reading of *Religion*. Furthermore, Firestone and Jacobs's use of the text extends only as far as defending its overall coherence. This contrasts with the position of interpreters such as Gordon Michaelson,* a scholar of religious thought, who see *Religion* as highlighting fundamental tensions and contradictions in Kant's moral philosophy and metaphysics. Moreover, in analyzing *Religion*, Firestone and Jacobs offer the disclaimer that they are not "commending its desirability for Christianity."[9]

It remains to be seen if similar interpreters will emerge to take this further step and become genuine advocates of the text.

NOTES

1   Immanuel Kant, *Religion within the Boundaries of Mere Reason*, trans. and ed. Allen Wood and George Di Giovanni (Cambridge: Cambridge University Press, 1998), 157.

2   Friedrich Schleiermacher, *On Religion: Speeches to Its Cultured Despisers* (Cambridge: Cambridge University Press, 1996), xv–xxiv.

3   Karl Barth, *The Epistle to the Romans* (London: Oxford University Press, 1933), 432.

4   Immanuel Kant, *Critique of Pure Reason*, trans. Paul Guyer and Allen Wood (Cambridge: Cambridge University Press, 1999).

5   Herbert Vorgrimmler, *Understanding Karl Rahner: An Introduction to His Life and Thought* (London: Epworth Press, 2012), 1–19.

6   Hermann Cohen, *Religion of Reason: Out of the Sources of Judaism* (New York: Oxford University Press USA, 1995).

7   Kant, *Religion*, 131.

8   See: Chris L. Firestone and Nathan Jacobs, *In Defense of Kant's Religion* (Bloomington: Indiana University Press, 2008).

9   Firestone and Jacobs, *In Defense*, 6.

MODULE 11
IMPACT AND INFLUENCE TODAY

KEY POINTS

- Most of the current study of *Religion* places it within the historical development of Enlightenment* thought. Influential thinkers such as G. W. F. Hegel* and the German economist and political philosopher Karl Marx* subsequently modified Kant's ideas, obscuring Kant's original meaning.

- The field of moral philosophy* remains closely tied to some of Kant's ideas. But his emphasis on the necessity of a God that we cannot hope to understand has fallen out of favor.

- Most scholars feel no need to combine theological arguments with contemporary philosophy today. *Religion* therefore remains useful primarily as an example of a moral philosophy based on religion.

Position

Immanuel Kant's *Religion within the Boundaries of Mere Reason* owes much to his earlier works. Two ideas found in *Critique of Pure Reason* (1781), for example, have special relevance to the work. First, Kant's "Transcendental Dialectic,"* the second of the two principal sections of Kant's *Critique of Pure Reason*, stated that any theories relating to theological concepts such as God or the soul were impossible. Second, he contended that autonomous beings required a belief in God and the immortality of the soul to sustain themselves in their moral endeavors. We may find this complex relationship between morality and religion throughout *Religion*. The very ambiguity of

> ❝ All human knowledge begins with intuitions, proceeds from thence to concepts, and ends with ideas. ❞
>
> Immanuel Kant, *Critique of Pure Reason*

the position has subjected the text to both negative and positive assessments since its publication.

Understanding *Religion*'s significance today requires us to understand those it most heavily influenced. Of the first major post-Kantian philosophers, G. W. F. Hegel in particular rejected Kant's suggestion that some things were unknowable. Hegel introduced his concept of the Absolute* in his work *Phenomenology of Spirit* (1807).[1] We should not see Hegel's work as a rejection of Kant but, rather, as a modification of his ideas. Hegel's important work has had a profound effect on how scholars view Kant's theories, even those based on *Religion*.

Later in the nineteenth century, the German economist and political philosopher Karl Marx was heavily indebted to Hegel as he formed the concepts that became socialism. Marx took the transcendental dialectic to a new level, introducing the idea of dialectical* materialism, a complex concept that led to a rejection of the existence of God. It would be difficult to overstate the influence of Marxism* on the history of the world.

Critics frequently charge that Kant's idea that central concepts of religion are not objects of theoretical knowledge dealt a blow to the concepts underlying religion and theology. It is true, however, that Kant clearly wanted to find a place for religion within his thought. The way he tied religious doctrines to the phenomena of hope, moral despair, freedom, and natural beauty opened avenues for using critical philosophy to help understand theological metaphysics.* The philosopher Friedrich Schleiermacher,* for example, although deeply influenced by Kant, understood religion to be a question of a feeling of dependence on God rather than a matter of theoretical proofs. Later in the nineteenth century, the Danish philosopher Søren Kierkegaard* would also locate religious and everyday moral and political experience beyond the constriction of theoretical proofs.

Interaction

Religion may be of interest to those working on Kant's philosophy and those engaged in the history of Enlightenment religious thought. The dominant tendency throughout much of the twentieth century was to examine *Religion* as a guide to Kant's moral philosophy rather as an account of his theology. Behind this order of priority lay at least two related phenomena.

First, philosophy became predominantly secular in the twentieth century. Second, influential presentations of Kant as an epistemologist* rather than a metaphysician*—roughly, someone conducting inquiry into the nature of knowledge rather than questions concerning the nature of being—sparked a revival of interest in Kant's theoretical philosophy in the latter half of that period.

Important Kantian ethicists have attempted sympathetic expositions of his religious thought nevertheless. The US philosopher Allen Wood,* for example, has written seminal accounts of this area of Kant's work.[2] The British philosopher and politician Onora O'Neill's* "Tanner Lectures" also represented an attempt to take seriously the dimension of religious hope in Kant's thought.[3] Both scholars see *Religion* as an attempt to give a rendering of traditional religion in the terms of critical ethics.

A recent trend in Kant scholarship argues that these more modern interpretations reflect our contemporary preconceptions to a greater extent than they do Kant's intentions and the real spirit of the text. Chris Firestone* and Nathan Jacob's* book *In Defense of Kant's Religion* offers a "theologically affirmative" reading of Kant, for instance.[4] Kant saw himself as reacting against traditional, especially Protestant, Christian doctrine. But some modern scholars read Kant's conceptions of God and faith as consistent with Church teachings. And they argue for his use of scripture* as more than just a way to present his ethics.

The Continuing Debate

In recent times, the idea that Kantian ethics *requires* a theological element has taken root. The British philosopher and ethicist John Hare's* *The Moral Gap* examined what we may think of as the overriding structural problem of *Religion*: as moral beings we are placed under unconditional obligations that we do not have the capacity to fulfill.[5] However, Hare endorses Kant's argument that we can resolve the problem through religious hope, exploring the ways in which contemporary philosophy fails to confront or solve the problem in non-religious terms.

Hare focuses on what he sees as three inadequate responses to the structural problem of *Religion* that mainstream moral philosophy has adopted. First, he cites the exaggeration of our moral capacities; second, the downplaying of the strength of our moral obligations; and third, the finding of alternatives to divine assistance in natural processes.

He sees the first response at work in several utilitarian* theories that require moral deliberations to be impartial to guarantee the greatest good for the greatest number of people (according to utilitarian thought, the "best" action is the action that causes the greatest good for the greatest number of people). Hare contends that such impartiality is impossible. He sees the second response at work in feminist philosophy, which disputes the Kantian idea that moral demands have a universal scope. Hare concedes that some important moral demands apply to particular groups or communities, but argues that this does not remove our universal obligations to others or diminish their strength.

As for natural replacements for divine assistance, Hare challenges evolutionary (and other) theories on how egotistic tendencies become harnessed over time for—or transformed into—forms of social cooperation. Hare adopts Kant's solution that human beings require divine assistance to become the moral agents we used to be. He therefore advocates doctrines of atonement* and justificatory grace.*

NOTES

1   Georg Wilhelm Friedrich Hegel, Phenomenology of Spirit, trans. A. V. Miller (Oxford: Oxford University Press, 1977).

2   Allen W. Wood, *Kant's Rational Theology* (Ithaca and London: Cornell University Press, 1978); Allen W. Wood, *Kant's Moral Religion* (Ithaca and London: Cornell University Press, 1970).

3   Onora O'Neill, "*Kant on Reason and Religion,*" in *The Tanner Lectures on Human Values, 1997*, ed. Grethe B. Patterson (Salt Lake City: University of Utah Press, 1997), 269–308.

4   Chris L. Firestone and Nathan Jacobs, *In Defense of Kant's Religion* (Bloomington: Indiana University Press, 2008).

5   John E. Hare, *The Moral Gap: Kantian Ethics, Human Limits, and God's Assistance* (Oxford: Clarendon Press, 1996).

WHERE NEXT?

KEY POINTS

- Kant's religious thoughts have been eclipsed by his more influential critical works.

- *Religion* remains an important text in the growing field of the philosophy of religion.*

- Kant's entire body of work was an attempt to explain the human condition. *Religion* should be seen as a part of that process and one that delves into important areas of morality and ethics.

Potential

For many of Immanuel Kant's first readers, the religious ideas put forward in *Religion within the Boundaries of Mere Reason* were central to the great appeal of his philosophy. But in the two centuries since Kant's death, his religious thought has moved from the center to the periphery of Kant's perceived relevance. He remains one of the most frequently studied philosophers, but today scholars are most interested in his contributions to moral philosophy,* aesthetics,* epistemology,* and metaphysics* as set out in his three great *Critiques*.*¹ Kant set out his moral arguments for belief in God and the immortality of the soul in his main work in moral philosophy, the *Critique of Practical Reason* (1788).² Yet scholars have neglected his more explicit engagements with the theology in *Religion*. And that has been true for at least the past century.

Western philosophy has grown more secular since Kant's time, with theology becoming, for the most part, a separate discipline. *Religion*'s deep engagement with biblical themes and historical

> ❝Dare to think!❞
>
> Immanuel Kant, "An Answer to the Question, What Is Enlightenment?"

theology makes it a peculiar text for contemporary moral philosophers. The work seems very much a product of its time. Indeed, even certain contemporaries of Kant found *Religion*'s apparent indebtedness to theological tradition to be disappointingly backward-looking. The nineteenth-century German philosopher Friedrich Nietzsche* found it ironic that Kant, who did so much to dismantle the intellectual legitimacy of theological metaphysics, wrote a work that attempted to rescue traditional theological ideas.

Future Directions

Religion had become rather irrelevant in twentieth-century English-speaking philosophy. One factor that has renewed interest in Kant is the possibility of reading him as an epistemologist with minimal metaphysical commitments. Interpreters such as the British philosopher Peter Strawson* have related Kant to the anti-metaphysical orientation of twentieth-century philosophy. Yet this reading reduces the likelihood that *Religion* will receive renewed attention. At first glance it seems to be a particularly metaphysical text, not only because it uses traditional religious ideas, but also because it frequently appeals to such puzzling entities as the "supersensible self"* (roughly, that part of a person that exists beyond what our senses can perceive).

Nevertheless, in the past few years we have seen an increase in philosophical writing on Kant's religious thought in general and on *Religion* in particular. One factor behind this shift may be an increasingly sympathetic attitude to metaphysics and, therefore, to more metaphysical interpretations of Kant. Another factor has undoubtedly been the steady growth in the sub-discipline of philosophy of religion. Because of the ways in which it develops certain themes in Kant's practical thought, *Religion* continues to be a source of ideas for those working in Kantian moral philosophy—a field that grows larger and more influential each year. While philosophers with more religious inclinations are also beginning to produce examinations of the text, this activity lies outside the mainstream. And these scholars do not necessarily endorse the work's content. Kant's other works have no shortage of committed advocates today. Whether *Religion* will in the future enjoy anything like that status depends at least in part on whether philosophy and theology become more closely aligned. At present, the prospects for such an alignment remain rather bleak.

Summary

While it has not had anything like the influence of the *Critiques*, Kant's *Religion within the Boundaries of Mere Reason* remains a fascinating and endlessly puzzling text. Its nature and rationale appear strange to many of its readers today. Even Kant's contemporaries found it surprising. His late-in-life engagement with the Bible and the themes of Christian theology seemed uncharacteristic for a leading figure of the late Enlightenment.* He advocated such common Enlightenment themes as freedom of religious expression and skepticism about the structures, authority, and practices of the Church. And contemporary scholars widely regarded his philosophy as having struck the most sophisticated, systematic, and devastating blow to theology, especially as a discipline making metaphysical claims. Furthermore, Kant insisted that morality was based upon reason and the autonomy of the individual.

Any religious claim would have to submit to the jury of human reason. And religion could not lay claim to have any more moral validity than a man's unaided rational thoughts. It puzzled his contemporaries—and it continues to puzzle scholars and critics today—that the man who produced these radical theories should publish a work that, at least on the surface, seeks to establish concord with traditional theological concepts.

Today, Kantian moral philosophy has a striking number of defenders. Kantianism is usually characterized by an attempt at general loyalty, albeit not a slavish one, to Kant's texts. *Religion* presents a set of challenges to today's broadly secular brand of moral philosophy. Why should ideas of evil, grace,* and providence* have been so important to Kant's philosophy of autonomy? Can one interpret the text as dispensing with theology altogether, or at least as domesticating theology within philosophical terms? Some interpreters, both religious and secular, contend that the text points broadly to the religious character of Kant's thought. This presents problems for the current industry of secular Kantian moral philosophy and perhaps for moral philosophy more generally as an independent practice.

Regardless of one's own interpretation, Kant remains perhaps the most significant philosopher of the Enlightenment. And the way he combined a moral philosophy grounded on human freedom with biblical and theological exploration makes *Religion* a work of abiding interest.

NOTES

1   Immanuel Kant, *Critique of Practical Reason, Critique of Pure Reason, Critique on the Power of Judgment.*

2   Immanuel Kant, *Critique of Practical Reason*, trans. Mary McGregor (Cambridge: Cambridge University Press, 1997).

GLOSSARIES

GLOSSARY OF TERMS

Absolute: for the philosopher G. W. F. Hegel, the Absolute was that which was independent and unchanging; an absolute truth is inherently unknowable, though the process of attempting to understand it can aid in our understanding of the whole.

Absolute idealism: an idea attributed to the philosopher G. W. F. Hegel. Its chief difference from Kant's version of the philosophy of idealism is that Hegel rejected the notion that certain ideas were unknowable. According to Hegel, a complex process was required to grasp what he called the Absolute or "everything." Only by understanding the Absolute could one truly understand anything.

Aesthetics: a subdiscipline of philosophy concerned broadly with the nature of beauty, art, and judgments of taste. The word derives from the Greek term for sensory perception.

A priori: a Latin term Kant used to describe a thought process. Kant argued that although all thought began with experience it did not necessarily arise from experience. *A priori* thought is transcendental and, therefore, separate from more empirical thoughts (that is, thoughts derived from experience).

Atonement: in Christian theology, the doctrine that God and sinful man become reconciled by means of the death and resurrection of Jesus Christ, through which sins are forgiven or mankind is redeemed. The atonement continues to be a controversial theme in Christian theology. Different Christian denominations subscribe to different versions of the doctrine.

Catholicism: also known as Roman Catholicism, a Christian religion that follows the teachings and structure of Christianity's classical origins. The pope is the supreme authority of this religion.

Counterfeit service: Kant's term for the rituals that signify "faith," which serve as obstacles to true moral faith.

Critique: a word with a technical sense for Kant, which need not have the negative connotations it carries in common usage. By "critique," Kant means an investigation into the grounds for, and the limits of, any *a priori* principle claimed by human knowledge.

Deterministic: philosophical term describing an effect that is the inevitable consequence of preceding events.

Dialectic: a method of resolving an argument between two viewpoints to ascertain the truth. Though the dialectic itself is a concept that stretches back to ancient Greek times, Kant, G. W. F. Hegel, and Karl Marx developed the idea further.

Empiricism: a position in the theory of knowledge that holds that all knowledge derives from sensory experience. The most famous British empiricists are John Locke, George Berkeley, and David Hume.

Enlightenment: a cultural and intellectual movement that took place in seventeenth- and eighteenth-century Europe and North America. The movement was devoted to combating irrationality, superstition, and arbitrary political authority.

Epistemology: the philosophical study of the nature of knowledge and the justification of belief.

Ethical commonwealth: Kant's idea of a more perfect world where people would be united by non-coercive, self-regulated laws in a virtuous kingdom.

Ethics: the philosophical study, also known as moral philosophy, of the concepts of right and wrong.

Evolutionary biology: the study of the evolution of species over a long period of time.

French Revolution (1789–99): a period of political and social upheaval that culminated in the execution of Louis XVI and the drafting of several transitory, more democratic, constitutions.

Grace: in Christian theology, some form of freely offered love, mercy, or benevolence bestowed by God on human beings. Christian tradition has distinguished many kinds of grace and articulated many views about its nature and effectiveness. These differences play a prominent role in distinguishing the theologies of different Christian denominations.

Heaven: a concept, also known as the Kingdom of God, that features in both the Old and New Testaments. It is a central part of Jesus' teaching and also discussed by St. Paul (one of the founders of the Christian Church). Heaven plays a role in the study of the end of human history, or the destiny of mankind.

Idealism: a philosophy that emphasizes the idea that reality as we know it is constructed in the mind or is otherwise immaterial.

Kingdom of God: also known as "heaven," a feature of both the Old and New Testaments. The concept plays a major part in the teachings of Jesus and is discussed by St. Paul; it figures heavily in ideas of the destiny of mankind.

Königsberg: Initially in Prussia, the city became part of Germany after unification in 1871. In 1946 the Soviet Union annexed it and renamed it Kaliningrad. It remains a Russian possession today.

Leibnizian-Wolffian: a rationalist school of philosophy based upon the writings of the philosophers Gottfried Wilhelm von Leibniz and Christian Wolff. It enjoyed widespread popularity in German philosophy prior to Kant. The German philosopher Leibniz was a key figure in the rationalist movement of early modern philosophy. Christian Wolff was a German philosopher who argued that truth could be discovered only by using reason and concise methodology.

Lutheranism: a protestant Christian denomination based on the works of the sixteenth-century German theologian Martin Luther.

Marxism: the name ascribed to the political system advocated by Karl Marx. It emphasized an end to capitalism by taking control of the means of production from individuals and placing it firmly in the hands of central government.

Metaphysics: the philosophical study of the ultimate nature of reality or being. In Kant's day, it embraced "general metaphysics," or "ontology," and "special metaphysics." The latter concerns the nature of specific entities that Kant believed transcend the limits of human experience, namely the world, the soul, and God.

Moral philosophy: also known as ethics, a branch of philosophy concerned with understanding and explaining notions of right and wrong.

New Testament: the second part of the Christian Bible describing the life and thought of Jesus Christ.

Original sin: a doctrine in Christian theology that attributes the sinful nature of humanity to Adam and Eve's disobedience in the Garden of Eden. The nature of the resulting sin as well as the extent of humanity's guilt is traditionally a matter of considerable controversy.

Pantheism: a position within theology and philosophy that identifies God with all reality. A prominent historical representative of pantheism was the Dutch philosopher Benedictus Spinoza, who identified God and nature.

Pantheism controversy: a debate in the field of philosophy that stemmed from a 1780 conversation between the philosophers Friedrich Heinrich Jacobi and Gotthold Lessing. This inspired Jacobi to engage in a protracted study of Benedictus Spinoza. As Spinoza's work emphasized materialism, Jacobi decided its logical conclusion was atheism since, clearly, God had no substance and was not material.

Pietism: a Lutheran reform movement that began in the seventeenth century and became highly influential in the eighteenth century. It stressed personal piety, religious experience, and the role of conscience in the religious life.

Philosophy of religion: any attempt to use philosophical thought to either confirm or deny the existence of a divine being. It is considered a separate field from theology.

Protestantism: one of the two principle branches of Christianity. Protestants reject many of the doctrines of the Catholic Church, notably the meaning of certain rituals, and the status of the Catholic Pope.

Providence: in theology, God's involvement in nature and history. It concerns God's general maintenance and sustenance of the world, God's guidance or direction of human history, as well as God's particular interventions.

Prussia: a former nation with the Duchy of Prussia at its heart that was part of the Holy Roman Empire (a loose collection of central European states that was dissolved in 1806 shortly after the Battle of Jena). Prussia rose to prominence as a major power in the seventeenth century; its capital was Königsberg until 1701, when the government moved to Berlin. The Prussian state was instrumental in unifying Germany in 1871.

Rational autonomy: a theory that rational human beings have control over their actions in the world—moral autonomy. For Kant, true freedom requires transcendental freedom, the will's ability to determine actions independently of the influence of the mechanical causes that govern nature.

Rationalism: a philosophical school in seventeenth- and eighteenth-century Europe. The rationalists gave their philosophical proofs a rigorous, quasi-mathematical structure and believed, unlike the empiricists, that some knowledge was innate to human reason. The most important rationalists were René Descartes, Benedictus Spinoza, and Gottfried Wilhelm von Leibniz.

Redemption: a Christian doctrine according to which an individual receives forgiveness for the sins he or she has committed. In the Christian religion, redemption can help one avoid damnation to eternal hell.

Reformation: the event in which the Protestant Church split from the Catholic Church, principally over matters of doctrine. The Protestant minister Martin Luther was one of the Reformation's key figures.

Revelation-based theology: the study of God or a religion based on communication with a divine being.

Romanticism: an intellectual movement that often found expression in art and literature. The movement began in Germany around the beginning of the nineteenth century and emphasized emotion as the source of aesthetics.

Rosicrucianism: a secret society claiming to possess esoteric spiritual and religious knowledge. It was founded in medieval Germany, supposedly by Christian Rosenkreuz, who was most probably an allegorical figure.

Scholasticism: a medieval tradition of education that emphasizes dialectical reasoning. This type of thinking would be used to discover contradictions by inferring truths from observations of new or prior thought.

Scripture: usually refers to some kind of holy text or book, most commonly the Christian Bible.

Supersensible self: the part of a person that exists beyond what our senses can perceive. Heaven, for example, is a supersensible realm and those who "live" there would be considered supersensible entities.

Theology: the discipline devoted to explaining the nature of God or the divine as well as the doctrines of religions quite generally.

Thomism: the philosophical school that stems from the work of the medieval theologian St. Thomas Aquinas. His seminal text *Summa Theologica* is one of the most influential works of medieval theology.

Transcendental dialectic: the second of the two main sections of Kant's *Critique of Pure Reason*. In this section, Kant attempts to describe what he terms the "dialectical" nature of pure human reason—how it falls into contradictions of its own making when it attempts to transcend experience and form concepts of the soul, God, and the cosmos.

Utilitarianism: the theory in moral philosophy according to which actions or principles are good if they maximize utility. Usually, this is interpreted to mean those generating the greatest good for the greatest number of people.

PEOPLE MENTIONED IN THE TEXT

Thomas Aquinas (1225–74) was a medieval philosopher and theologian. His seminal text *Summa Theologica* (1265–74) is one of the most influential works of medieval theology.

Karl Barth (1886–1968) was a Swiss Reformed theologian. He is known for his thirteen-volume *Church Dogmatics* (1932–67).

Ernst Cassirer (1874–1945) was a German philosopher of the Neo-Kantian School. He was mentored by the philosopher Hermann Cohen, but departed from Cohen's work when he developed his theory of symbolism.

Hermann Cohen (1842–1918) was a German Jewish philosopher and one of the founders of the Marburg school of Neo-Kantianism. His works include *Kant's Theory of Experience* (1871) and *Religion of Reason out of the Sources of Judaism* (1919).

Charles Darwin (1809–82) was an English natural historian. His work on the theory of evolution by natural selection, *On the Origin of Species* (1859), is considered to be one of the most important and influential books of all time.

René Descartes (1596–1650) was a French rationalist philosopher and mathematician, best known for inventing Cartesian coordinates and his discussion around the statement "cogito ergo sum" (I think, therefore I am).

Ludwig Feuerbach (1804–72) was a German Hegelian philosopher. He is most widely known for the critique of religion in his work *The Essence of Christianity* (1841). Feuerbach claimed that belief in a transcendent deity involved a process of projection of humanity's "species being" onto a fictional entity. Feuerbach's arguments drew largely upon Hegel's philosophy, especially upon the section of the *Phenomenology* entitled "Stoicism, Skepticism, and the Unhappy Consciousnesses."

Johann Gottlieb Fichte (1762–1814) was the first of the three major philosophers of German idealism, the others being Schelling and Hegel. Hegel regarded Fichte's philosophy as a natural extension of Kant's and as a necessary step toward the true philosophical system Hegel himself had set out to write. Fichte introduced the idea of mutual recognition that is central to Hegel's *Phenomenology*.

Robert Filmer (1588–1653) was an English political thinker whose major works include the book *Patriarcha* (1680), which argues that royal power is absolute. Consequently, he maintains that in society all people are bound to obey and submit to the monarch.

Chris Firestone is a professor of philosophy and chair of the philosophy department at Trinity International University in Deerfield, Illinois.

Friedrich II (1712–86) also known as Frederick the Great, ruled Prussia between 1740 and 1786. He was interested in philosophy and was a patron of both the arts and the Enlightenment, in stark contrast to his successor and son Friedrich Wilhelm II, who opposed Enlightenment ideals with great vigor.

Friedrich Wilhelm I (1688–1740) was the King of Prussia from 1713 to 1740 and has sometimes been named the "soldier king." He is known for his military and agricultural reforms, his autocratic style of ruling and his successful economic management of the country.

Friedrich Wilhelm II (1744–97) was the king of Prussia from 1786 until his death in 1797. He was politically conservative. Kant wrote *Religion within the Boundaries of Mere Reason* partly in response to the king's attitudes toward censorship.

Sigmund Freud (1856–1939) was an Austrian physician and psychologist who is regarded as the founder of psychoanalysis. His works include *The Interpretation of Dreams* (1899).

Johann Wolfgang von Goethe (1749–1832) was a German writer, politician, and scientist and author of the play *Faust*.

John E. Hare (b. 1949) is a British academic who specializes in the field of ethics. He is currently Noah Porter Professor of Philosophical Theology at Yale Divinity School.

Georg Wilhelm Friedrich Hegel (1770–1831) was the preeminent philosopher of German idealism and the author of works including *Phenomenology of Spirit* (1807) and *Science of Logic* (1812–16).

Johann Gottfried von Herder (1744–1803) was a German philosopher, poet, and theologian. He is considered an important Enlightenment thinker.

Thomas Hobbes (1588–1679) was an English philosopher best remembered for his book *Leviathan* (1651), in which he established what is now known as social contract theory. Hobbes championed government, specifically the monarchy, as the supreme defense against the chaotic "state of nature."

David Hume (1711–76) was a Scottish empiricist philosopher and historian. His philosophy is most extensively elaborated in *A Treatise of Human Nature* (1739).

Nathan A. Jacobs is a visiting scholar and lecturer of philosophy at the University of Kentucky. He formerly held the post of assistant professor of religion and philosophy at John Brown University.

Søren Kierkegaard (1813–55) was a Danish Protestant philosopher and theologian. His works include *Either/Or* (1843) and *Fear and Trembling* (1843).

Martin Knutzen (1713–51) was a German philosopher who is best remembered as one of Immanuel Kant's teachers.

Gottfried Wilhelm von Leibniz (1646–1716) was a German philosopher and a key figure in the rationalist movement of early modern philosophy. A hugely prolific author, he is known for his *Monadology* (1714) and *Theodicy* (1710).

Gotthold Ephraim Lessing (1729–81) was a German dramatist, critic, and philosopher. A central member of the German Enlightenment, his works include the play *Nathan the Wise* (1779).

Martin Luther (1483–1546) was a German theologian and religious reformer who inspired the Protestant Reformation. His 1518 work *95 Theses* was one of the first to benefit from the invention of the printing press.

Karl Marx (1818–83) was a German philosopher, political theorist, and economist. Marx was the major historical theorist of communism, and his prodigious output includes *Das Kapital* (1867).

Moses Mendelssohn (1729–86) was a German philosopher. The chief figure of the so-called *Haskalah,* the Jewish Enlightenment of the eighteenth century, he is the author of *Jerusalem* (1783) and *Phädon or On the Immortality of Souls* (1767).

Gordon Michaelson is a professor of the humanities at the New College of Florida. He specializes in religious thought in the Western world from the Enlightenment to the present.

Isaac Newton (1642–1726) was an English physicist and mathematician. Among his many contributions to science, his laws of motion and theories of gravity remain the most important.

Friedrich Nietzsche (1844–1900) was a German philosopher and philologist. His works include *The Birth of Tragedy* (1872) and *Beyond Good and Evil* (1886).

Onora O'Neill (b. 1941) is a British philosopher, emeritus professor of philosophy at the University of Cambridge and a member of the House of Lords in the British Parliament.

Karl Rahner (1904–84) was a German Jesuit priest and theologian. His works include *Spirit in the World* (1968) and *The Trinity* (1970).

Friedrich Wilhelm Joseph von Schelling (1775–1854) was a German idealist philosopher. A roommate of Hegel's in the Tübingen seminary, the two collaborated on a common philosophical project. The publication of Hegel's *Phenomenology*, with its stinging critiques of Schelling, signaled that each would follow his own separate path. Schelling's output was prolific. His main works during the period when Hegel was developing his own positions were *Ideas for a Philosophy of Nature: as Introduction to the Study of this Science* (1797), *System of Transcendental Idealism* (1800), and *Bruno, or On the Natural and the Divine Principle of Things* (1802).

Friedrich Schleiermacher (1768–1834) was a German theologian, philosopher, and translator. His works include *On Religion: Speeches to its Cultured Despisers* (1799).

Benedictus Spinoza (1632–77) was a Dutch philosopher and major representative of early-modern rationalism. His works include *Ethics* (1677) and *Tractatus Theologico-Politicus* (1670).

Karl Friedrich Stäudlin (1761–1826) was a theology professor at the University of Göttingen. He specialized in the fields of Church history and moral philosophy.

Peter Frederick Strawson (1919–2006) was a British philosopher and professor of metaphysical philosophy at the University of Oxford (Magdalen College) from 1968 to 1987.

Voltaire (1694–1778) was the pen name of François-Marie Arouet, a philosopher and historian associated with the French Enlightenment. Famous for his attacks on the Catholic Church and his advocacy of freedom of religion and expression, his works include the novel *Candide* (1759).

Christian Wolff (1679–1754) was a German philosopher. A disciple of Leibniz and expositor of his works, Wolff is little read today. He was, however, a major force in eighteenth-century German philosophy and author of a vast number of works on most of the scholarly subjects of his day.

Johann Christoph von Wöllner (1732–1800) was one of Friedrich Wilhelm II's ministers. Like the king, Wöllner was a Rosicrucian.

Allen W. Wood (b. 1942) is an American academic and Ruth Norman Halls Professor of Philosophy at Indiana University. He specializes in the study of the works of Immanuel Kant.

WORKS CITED

WORKS CITED

Barth, Karl. *The Epistle to the Romans.* London: Oxford University Press,1933.

Bubbio, Paulo Diego, and Paul Redding. *Religion after Kant: God and Culture in the Idealist Era.* Newcastle: Cambridge Scholars Publishing, 2012.

Cassirer, Ernst. *Kant's Life and Thought.* Translated by James Haden, with an introduction by Stephan Körner. New Haven: Yale University Press, 1981.

Cohen, Hermann. *Religion of Reason: Out of the Sources of Judaism.* New York: Oxford University Press USA, 1995.

Firestone, Chris L., and Jacobs, Nathan. *In Defense of Kant's Religion.* Bloomington: Indiana University Press, 2008.

Ford, Guy Stanton. "Wöllner and the Prussian Religious Edict of 1788." *The American Historical Review* 15, no. 3 (1910).

Hare, John E. *The Moral Gap: Kantian Ethics, Human Limits, and God's Assistance.* Oxford: Clarendon Press, 1996.

Hegel, Georg Wilhelm Friedrich. *Phenomenology of Spirit.* Translated by A. V. Miller. Oxford: Oxford University Press, 1977.

Insole, Christopher J. *Kant and the Creation of Freedom: A Theological Problem.* Oxford: Oxford University Press, 2013.

Kant, Immanuel. "An Answer to the Question: What Is Enlightenment?" In *Cambridge Texts in the History of Political Thought.* Ed. H.S.Reiss. Trans. H. B.Nisbet. Cambridge: Cambridge University Press, 1991.

———. "Conjectural Beginning of Human History." In *Anthropology, History, and Education*, edited by Robert B. Louden and Günter Zöller. Cambridge: Cambridge University Press, 2011, 160–75.

———. *Correspondence.* Translated and edited by Arnulf Zweig. Cambridge: Cambridge University Press, 1999.

———. *Critique of Practical Reason.* Cambridge: Cambridge University Press, 1997.

———. *Critique of Pure Reason.* Translated by Paul Guyer and Allen Wood. Cambridge: Cambridge University Press, 1999.

———. *Groundwork of the Metaphysics of Morals.* In *Cambridge Texts in the History of* Philosophy. Cambridge: Cambridge University Press, 2012.

———. "Idea for a Universal History with a Cosmopolitan Aim." In *Anthropology, History, and Education*, edited by Robert B. Louden and Günter

Zöller. Cambridge: Cambridge University Press, 2011, 107–20.

_____. *On the Old Saw: That May be Right in Principle but it Won't Work in Practice.* Translated by E. B. Ashton. Pennsylvania: University of Pennsylvania Press, 1974.

_____. *Opus Postumum* in *The Cambridge Edition of the Works of Immanual Kant.* Edited by Eckart Förster and Michael Rosen. Cambridge: Cambridge University Press, 1995.

— — —. "Perpetual Peace." New York: Cosimo, 2005.

— — —. *Religion and Rational Theology.* Edited and translated by Allen Wood and George Di Giovanni. Cambridge: Cambridge University Press, 1996.

— — —. *Religion within the Boundaries of Mere Reason.* Translated and edited by Allen Wood and George Di Giovanni. Cambridge: Cambridge University Press, 1998.

_____. *The Conflict of the Faculties.* Translated by Mary J. McGregor. Nebraska: University of Nebraska Press, 1992.

_____. *Thoughts on the True Estimation of Living Forces*

— — —. "What Does It Mean to Orient Oneself in Thinking?" In *Religion and Rational Theology*, edited and translated by Allen Wood and George Di Giovanni. Cambridge: Cambridge University Press, 1996, 1–18.

Kuehn, Manfred. *Kant: A Biography.* Cambridge: Cambridge University Press, 2001.

Lessing, Gotthold Ephraim. "The Education of the Human Race." In *Literary and Philosophical Essays.* Edited by Charles W. Eliot. New York: P. F. Collier & Son, 1909–14.

Mariña, Jacqueline. "Kant on Grace: A Reply to his Critics." *Religious Studies* 33, no. 4 (1997): 379–400.

Mendelssohn, Moses. *Jerusalem: Or on Religious Power and Judaism.* Trans. Allan Arkush. Massachusetts: Brandeis University Press, 1983.

O'Neill, Onora. "Kant on Reason and Religion". In *The Tanner Lectures on Human Values, 1997*, edited by Grethe B. Patterson. Salt Lake City: University of Utah Press, 1997, 269–308.

Schleiermacher, Friedrich. *On Religion: Speeches to Its Cultured Despisers.* Cambridge: Cambridge University Press, 1996.

Vorgrimmler, Herbert. *Understanding Karl Rahner: An Introduction to His Life and Thought.* London: Epworth Press, 2012.

Wood, Allen W. *Kant's Moral Religion*. Ithaca and London: Cornell University Press, 1970.

_____. *Kant's Rational Theology*. Ithaca and London: Cornell University Press, 1978.

THE MACAT LIBRARY
BY DISCIPLINE

AFRICANA STUDIES

Chinua Achebe's *An Image of Africa: Racism in Conrad's Heart of Darkness*
W. E. B. Du Bois's *The Souls of Black Folk*
Zora Neale Huston's *Characteristics of Negro Expression*
Martin Luther King Jr's *Why We Can't Wait*
Toni Morrison's *Playing in the Dark: Whiteness in the American Literary Imagination*

ANTHROPOLOGY

Arjun Appadurai's *Modernity at Large: Cultural Dimensions of Globalisation*
Philippe Ariès's *Centuries of Childhood*
Franz Boas's *Race, Language and Culture*
Kim Chan & Renée Mauborgne's *Blue Ocean Strategy*
Jared Diamond's *Guns, Germs & Steel: the Fate of Human Societies*
Jared Diamond's *Collapse: How Societies Choose to Fail or Survive*
E. E. Evans-Pritchard's *Witchcraft, Oracles and Magic Among the Azande*
James Ferguson's *The Anti-Politics Machine*
Clifford Geertz's *The Interpretation of Cultures*
David Graeber's *Debt: the First 5000 Years*
Karen Ho's *Liquidated: An Ethnography of Wall Street*
Geert Hofstede's *Culture's Consequences: Comparing Values, Behaviors, Institutes and Organizations across Nations*
Claude Lévi-Strauss's *Structural Anthropology*
Jay Macleod's *Ain't No Makin' It: Aspirations and Attainment in a Low-Income Neighborhood*
Saba Mahmood's *The Politics of Piety: The Islamic Revival and the Feminist Subject*
Marcel Mauss's *The Gift*

BUSINESS

Jean Lave & Etienne Wenger's *Situated Learning*
Theodore Levitt's *Marketing Myopia*
Burton G. Malkiel's *A Random Walk Down Wall Street*
Douglas McGregor's *The Human Side of Enterprise*
Michael Porter's *Competitive Strategy: Creating and Sustaining Superior Performance*
John Kotter's *Leading Change*
C. K. Prahalad & Gary Hamel's *The Core Competence of the Corporation*

CRIMINOLOGY

Michelle Alexander's *The New Jim Crow: Mass Incarceration in the Age of Colorblindness*
Michael R. Gottfredson & Travis Hirschi's *A General Theory of Crime*
Richard Herrnstein & Charles A. Murray's *The Bell Curve: Intelligence and Class Structure in American Life*
Elizabeth Loftus's *Eyewitness Testimony*
Jay Macleod's *Ain't No Makin' It: Aspirations and Attainment in a Low-Income Neighborhood*
Philip Zimbardo's *The Lucifer Effect*

ECONOMICS

Janet Abu-Lughod's *Before European Hegemony*
Ha-Joon Chang's *Kicking Away the Ladder*
David Brion Davis's *The Problem of Slavery in the Age of Revolution*
Milton Friedman's *The Role of Monetary Policy*
Milton Friedman's *Capitalism and Freedom*
David Graeber's *Debt: the First 5000 Years*
Friedrich Hayek's *The Road to Serfdom*
Karen Ho's *Liquidated: An Ethnography of Wall Street*

John Maynard Keynes's *The General Theory of Employment, Interest and Money*
Charles P. Kindleberger's *Manias, Panics and Crashes*
Robert Lucas's *Why Doesn't Capital Flow from Rich to Poor Countries?*
Burton G. Malkiel's *A Random Walk Down Wall Street*
Thomas Robert Malthus's *An Essay on the Principle of Population*
Karl Marx's *Capital*
Thomas Piketty's *Capital in the Twenty-First Century*
Amartya Sen's *Development as Freedom*
Adam Smith's *The Wealth of Nations*
Nassim Nicholas Taleb's *The Black Swan: The Impact of the Highly Improbable*
Amos Tversky's & Daniel Kahneman's *Judgment under Uncertainty: Heuristics and Biases*
Mahbub Ul Haq's *Reflections on Human Development*
Max Weber's *The Protestant Ethic and the Spirit of Capitalism*

FEMINISM AND GENDER STUDIES

Judith Butler's *Gender Trouble*
Simone De Beauvoir's *The Second Sex*
Michel Foucault's *History of Sexuality*
Betty Friedan's *The Feminine Mystique*
Saba Mahmood's *The Politics of Piety: The Islamic Revival and the Feminist Subject*
Joan Wallach Scott's *Gender and the Politics of History*
Mary Wollstonecraft's *A Vindication of the Rights of Woman*
Virginia Woolf's *A Room of One's Own*

GEOGRAPHY

The Brundtland Report's *Our Common Future*
Rachel Carson's *Silent Spring*
Charles Darwin's *On the Origin of Species*
James Ferguson's *The Anti-Politics Machine*
Jane Jacobs's *The Death and Life of Great American Cities*
James Lovelock's *Gaia: A New Look at Life on Earth*
Amartya Sen's *Development as Freedom*
Mathis Wackernagel & William Rees's *Our Ecological Footprint*

HISTORY

Janet Abu-Lughod's *Before European Hegemony*
Benedict Anderson's *Imagined Communities*
Bernard Bailyn's *The Ideological Origins of the American Revolution*
Hanna Batatu's *The Old Social Classes And The Revolutionary Movements Of Iraq*
Christopher Browning's *Ordinary Men: Reserve Police Batallion 101 and the Final Solution in Poland*
Edmund Burke's *Reflections on the Revolution in France*
William Cronon's *Nature's Metropolis: Chicago And The Great West*
Alfred W. Crosby's *The Columbian Exchange*
Hamid Dabashi's *Iran: A People Interrupted*
David Brion Davis's *The Problem of Slavery in the Age of Revolution*
Nathalie Zemon Davis's *The Return of Martin Guerre*
Jared Diamond's *Guns, Germs & Steel: the Fate of Human Societies*
Frank Dikotter's *Mao's Great Famine*
John W Dower's *War Without Mercy: Race And Power In The Pacific War*
W. E. B. Du Bois's *The Souls of Black Folk*
Richard J. Evans's *In Defence of History*
Lucien Febvre's *The Problem of Unbelief in the 16th Century*
Sheila Fitzpatrick's *Everyday Stalinism*

The Macat Library By Discipline

Eric Foner's *Reconstruction: America's Unfinished Revolution, 1863-1877*
Michel Foucault's *Discipline and Punish*
Michel Foucault's *History of Sexuality*
Francis Fukuyama's *The End of History and the Last Man*
John Lewis Gaddis's *We Now Know: Rethinking Cold War History*
Ernest Gellner's *Nations and Nationalism*
Eugene Genovese's *Roll, Jordan, Roll: The World the Slaves Made*
Carlo Ginzburg's *The Night Battles*
Daniel Goldhagen's *Hitler's Willing Executioners*
Jack Goldstone's *Revolution and Rebellion in the Early Modern World*
Antonio Gramsci's *The Prison Notebooks*
Alexander Hamilton, John Jay & James Madison's *The Federalist Papers*
Christopher Hill's *The World Turned Upside Down*
Carole Hillenbrand's *The Crusades: Islamic Perspectives*
Thomas Hobbes's *Leviathan*
Eric Hobsbawm's *The Age Of Revolution*
John A. Hobson's *Imperialism: A Study*
Albert Hourani's *History of the Arab Peoples*
Samuel P. Huntington's *The Clash of Civilizations and the Remaking of World Order*
C. L. R. James's *The Black Jacobins*
Tony Judt's *Postwar: A History of Europe Since 1945*
Ernst Kantorowicz's *The King's Two Bodies: A Study in Medieval Political Theology*
Paul Kennedy's *The Rise and Fall of the Great Powers*
Ian Kershaw's *The "Hitler Myth": Image and Reality in the Third Reich*
John Maynard Keynes's *The General Theory of Employment, Interest and Money*
Charles P. Kindleberger's *Manias, Panics and Crashes*
Martin Luther King Jr's *Why We Can't Wait*
Henry Kissinger's *World Order: Reflections on the Character of Nations and the Course of History*
Thomas Kuhn's *The Structure of Scientific Revolutions*
Georges Lefebvre's *The Coming of the French Revolution*
John Locke's *Two Treatises of Government*
Niccolò Machiavelli's *The Prince*
Thomas Robert Malthus's *An Essay on the Principle of Population*
Mahmood Mamdani's *Citizen and Subject: Contemporary Africa And The Legacy Of Late Colonialism*
Karl Marx's *Capital*
Stanley Milgram's *Obedience to Authority*
John Stuart Mill's *On Liberty*
Thomas Paine's *Common Sense*
Thomas Paine's *Rights of Man*
Geoffrey Parker's *Global Crisis: War, Climate Change and Catastrophe in the Seventeenth Century*
Jonathan Riley-Smith's *The First Crusade and the Idea of Crusading*
Jean-Jacques Rousseau's *The Social Contract*
Joan Wallach Scott's *Gender and the Politics of History*
Theda Skocpol's *States and Social Revolutions*
Adam Smith's *The Wealth of Nations*
Timothy Snyder's *Bloodlands: Europe Between Hitler and Stalin*
Sun Tzu's *The Art of War*
Keith Thomas's *Religion and the Decline of Magic*
Thucydides's *The History of the Peloponnesian War*
Frederick Jackson Turner's *The Significance of the Frontier in American History*
Odd Arne Westad's *The Global Cold War: Third World Interventions And The Making Of Our Times*

LITERATURE

Chinua Achebe's *An Image of Africa: Racism in Conrad's Heart of Darkness*
Roland Barthes's *Mythologies*
Homi K. Bhabha's *The Location of Culture*
Judith Butler's *Gender Trouble*
Simone De Beauvoir's *The Second Sex*
Ferdinand De Saussure's *Course in General Linguistics*
T. S. Eliot's *The Sacred Wood: Essays on Poetry and Criticism*
Zora Neale Huston's *Characteristics of Negro Expression*
Toni Morrison's *Playing in the Dark: Whiteness in the American Literary Imagination*
Edward Said's *Orientalism*
Gayatri Chakravorty Spivak's *Can the Subaltern Speak?*
Mary Wollstonecraft's *A Vindication of the Rights of Women*
Virginia Woolf's *A Room of One's Own*

PHILOSOPHY

Elizabeth Anscombe's *Modern Moral Philosophy*
Hannah Arendt's *The Human Condition*
Aristotle's *Metaphysics*
Aristotle's *Nicomachean Ethics*
Edmund Gettier's *Is Justified True Belief Knowledge?*
Georg Wilhelm Friedrich Hegel's *Phenomenology of Spirit*
David Hume's *Dialogues Concerning Natural Religion*
David Hume's *The Enquiry for Human Understanding*
Immanuel Kant's *Religion within the Boundaries of Mere Reason*
Immanuel Kant's *Critique of Pure Reason*
Søren Kierkegaard's *The Sickness Unto Death*
Søren Kierkegaard's *Fear and Trembling*
C. S. Lewis's *The Abolition of Man*
Alasdair MacIntyre's *After Virtue*
Marcus Aurelius's *Meditations*
Friedrich Nietzsche's *On the Genealogy of Morality*
Friedrich Nietzsche's *Beyond Good and Evil*
Plato's *Republic*
Plato's *Symposium*
Jean-Jacques Rousseau's *The Social Contract*
Gilbert Ryle's *The Concept of Mind*
Baruch Spinoza's *Ethics*
Sun Tzu's *The Art of War*
Ludwig Wittgenstein's *Philosophical Investigations*

POLITICS

Benedict Anderson's *Imagined Communities*
Aristotle's *Politics*
Bernard Bailyn's *The Ideological Origins of the American Revolution*
Edmund Burke's *Reflections on the Revolution in France*
John C. Calhoun's *A Disquisition on Government*
Ha-Joon Chang's *Kicking Away the Ladder*
Hamid Dabashi's *Iran: A People Interrupted*
Hamid Dabashi's *Theology of Discontent: The Ideological Foundation of the Islamic Revolution in Iran*
Robert Dahl's *Democracy and its Critics*
Robert Dahl's *Who Governs?*
David Brion Davis's *The Problem of Slavery in the Age of Revolution*

The Macat Library By Discipline

Alexis De Tocqueville's *Democracy in America*
James Ferguson's *The Anti-Politics Machine*
Frank Dikotter's *Mao's Great Famine*
Sheila Fitzpatrick's *Everyday Stalinism*
Eric Foner's *Reconstruction: America's Unfinished Revolution, 1863-1877*
Milton Friedman's *Capitalism and Freedom*
Francis Fukuyama's *The End of History and the Last Man*
John Lewis Gaddis's *We Now Know: Rethinking Cold War History*
Ernest Gellner's *Nations and Nationalism*
David Graeber's *Debt: the First 5000 Years*
Antonio Gramsci's *The Prison Notebooks*
Alexander Hamilton, John Jay & James Madison's *The Federalist Papers*
Friedrich Hayek's *The Road to Serfdom*
Christopher Hill's *The World Turned Upside Down*
Thomas Hobbes's *Leviathan*
John A. Hobson's *Imperialism: A Study*
Samuel P. Huntington's *The Clash of Civilizations and the Remaking of World Order*
Tony Judt's *Postwar: A History of Europe Since 1945*
David C. Kang's *China Rising: Peace, Power and Order in East Asia*
Paul Kennedy's *The Rise and Fall of Great Powers*
Robert Keohane's *After Hegemony*
Martin Luther King Jr.'s *Why We Can't Wait*
Henry Kissinger's *World Order: Reflections on the Character of Nations and the Course of History*
John Locke's *Two Treatises of Government*
Niccolò Machiavelli's *The Prince*
Thomas Robert Malthus's *An Essay on the Principle of Population*
Mahmood Mamdani's *Citizen and Subject: Contemporary Africa And The Legacy Of Late Colonialism*
Karl Marx's *Capital*
John Stuart Mill's *On Liberty*
John Stuart Mill's *Utilitarianism*
Hans Morgenthau's *Politics Among Nations*
Thomas Paine's *Common Sense*
Thomas Paine's *Rights of Man*
Thomas Piketty's *Capital in the Twenty-First Century*
Robert D. Putman's *Bowling Alone*
John Rawls's *Theory of Justice*
Jean-Jacques Rousseau's *The Social Contract*
Theda Skocpol's *States and Social Revolutions*
Adam Smith's *The Wealth of Nations*
Sun Tzu's *The Art of War*
Henry David Thoreau's *Civil Disobedience*
Thucydides's *The History of the Peloponnesian War*
Kenneth Waltz's *Theory of International Politics*
Max Weber's *Politics as a Vocation*
Odd Arne Westad's *The Global Cold War: Third World Interventions And The Making Of Our Times*

POSTCOLONIAL STUDIES

Roland Barthes's *Mythologies*
Frantz Fanon's *Black Skin, White Masks*
Homi K. Bhabha's *The Location of Culture*
Gustavo Gutiérrez's *A Theology of Liberation*
Edward Said's *Orientalism*
Gayatri Chakravorty Spivak's *Can the Subaltern Speak?*

PSYCHOLOGY

Gordon Allport's *The Nature of Prejudice*
Alan Baddeley & Graham Hitch's *Aggression: A Social Learning Analysis*
Albert Bandura's *Aggression: A Social Learning Analysis*
Leon Festinger's *A Theory of Cognitive Dissonance*
Sigmund Freud's *The Interpretation of Dreams*
Betty Friedan's *The Feminine Mystique*
Michael R. Gottfredson & Travis Hirschi's *A General Theory of Crime*
Eric Hoffer's *The True Believer: Thoughts on the Nature of Mass Movements*
William James's *Principles of Psychology*
Elizabeth Loftus's *Eyewitness Testimony*
A. H. Maslow's *A Theory of Human Motivation*
Stanley Milgram's *Obedience to Authority*
Steven Pinker's *The Better Angels of Our Nature*
Oliver Sacks's *The Man Who Mistook His Wife For a Hat*
Richard Thaler & Cass Sunstein's *Nudge: Improving Decisions About Health, Wealth and Happiness*
Amos Tversky's *Judgment under Uncertainty: Heuristics and Biases*
Philip Zimbardo's *The Lucifer Effect*

SCIENCE

Rachel Carson's *Silent Spring*
William Cronon's *Nature's Metropolis: Chicago And The Great West*
Alfred W. Crosby's *The Columbian Exchange*
Charles Darwin's *On the Origin of Species*
Richard Dawkin's *The Selfish Gene*
Thomas Kuhn's *The Structure of Scientific Revolutions*
Geoffrey Parker's *Global Crisis: War, Climate Change and Catastrophe in the Seventeenth Century*
Mathis Wackernagel & William Rees's *Our Ecological Footprint*

SOCIOLOGY

Michelle Alexander's *The New Jim Crow: Mass Incarceration in the Age of Colorblindness*
Gordon Allport's *The Nature of Prejudice*
Albert Bandura's *Aggression: A Social Learning Analysis*
Hanna Batatu's *The Old Social Classes And The Revolutionary Movements Of Iraq*
Ha-Joon Chang's *Kicking Away the Ladder*
W. E. B. Du Bois's *The Souls of Black Folk*
Émile Durkheim's *On Suicide*
Frantz Fanon's *Black Skin, White Masks*
Frantz Fanon's *The Wretched of the Earth*
Eric Foner's *Reconstruction: America's Unfinished Revolution, 1863-1877*
Eugene Genovese's *Roll, Jordan, Roll: The World the Slaves Made*
Jack Goldstone's *Revolution and Rebellion in the Early Modern World*
Antonio Gramsci's *The Prison Notebooks*
Richard Herrnstein & Charles A Murray's *The Bell Curve: Intelligence and Class Structure in American Life*
Eric Hoffer's *The True Believer: Thoughts on the Nature of Mass Movements*
Jane Jacobs's *The Death and Life of Great American Cities*
Robert Lucas's *Why Doesn't Capital Flow from Rich to Poor Countries?*
Jay Macleod's *Ain't No Makin' It: Aspirations and Attainment in a Low Income Neighborhood*
Elaine May's *Homeward Bound: American Families in the Cold War Era*
Douglas McGregor's *The Human Side of Enterprise*
C. Wright Mills's *The Sociological Imagination*

The Macat Library By Discipline

Thomas Piketty's *Capital in the Twenty-First Century*
Robert D. Putman's *Bowling Alone*
David Riesman's *The Lonely Crowd: A Study of the Changing American Character*
Edward Said's *Orientalism*
Joan Wallach Scott's *Gender and the Politics of History*
Theda Skocpol's *States and Social Revolutions*
Max Weber's *The Protestant Ethic and the Spirit of Capitalism*

THEOLOGY

Augustine's *Confessions*
Benedict's *Rule of St Benedict*
Gustavo Gutiérrez's *A Theology of Liberation*
Carole Hillenbrand's *The Crusades: Islamic Perspectives*
David Hume's *Dialogues Concerning Natural Religion*
Immanuel Kant's *Religion within the Boundaries of Mere Reason*
Ernst Kantorowicz's *The King's Two Bodies: A Study in Medieval Political Theology*
Søren Kierkegaard's *The Sickness Unto Death*
C. S. Lewis's *The Abolition of Man*
Saba Mahmood's *The Politics of Piety: The Islamic Revival and the Feminist Subject*
Baruch Spinoza's *Ethics*
Keith Thomas's *Religion and the Decline of Magic*

COMING SOON

Chris Argyris's *The Individual and the Organisation*
Seyla Benhabib's *The Rights of Others*
Walter Benjamin's *The Work Of Art in the Age of Mechanical Reproduction*
John Berger's *Ways of Seeing*
Pierre Bourdieu's *Outline of a Theory of Practice*
Mary Douglas's *Purity and Danger*
Roland Dworkin's *Taking Rights Seriously*
James G. March's *Exploration and Exploitation in Organisational Learning*
Ikujiro Nonaka's *A Dynamic Theory of Organizational Knowledge Creation*
Griselda Pollock's *Vision and Difference*
Amartya Sen's *Inequality Re-Examined*
Susan Sontag's *On Photography*
Yasser Tabbaa's *The Transformation of Islamic Art*
Ludwig von Mises's *Theory of Money and Credit*

Macat Disciplines

Access the greatest ideas and thinkers across entire disciplines, including

AFRICANA STUDIES

Chinua Achebe's *An Image of Africa: Racism in Conrad's Heart of Darkness*

W. E. B. Du Bois's *The Souls of Black Folk*

Zora Neale Hurston's *Characteristics of Negro Expression*

Martin Luther King Jr.'s *Why We Can't Wait*

Toni Morrison's *Playing in the Dark: Whiteness in the American Literary Imagination*

Macat analyses are available from all good bookshops and libraries.

Access hundreds of analyses through one, multimedia tool.
Join free for one month **library.macat.com**

Macat Disciplines

Access the greatest ideas and thinkers across entire disciplines, including

FEMINISM, GENDER AND QUEER STUDIES

Simone De Beauvoir's
The Second Sex

Michel Foucault's
History of Sexuality

Betty Friedan's
The Feminine Mystique

Saba Mahmood's
*The Politics of Piety:
The Islamic Revival and
the Feminist Subject*

Joan Wallach Scott's
*Gender and the
Politics of History*

Mary Wollstonecraft's
*A Vindication of the
Rights of Woman*

Virginia Woolf's
A Room of One's Own

Judith Butler's
Gender Trouble

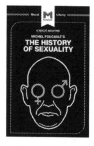

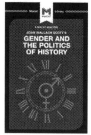

Macat analyses are available from all good bookshops and libraries.

Access hundreds of analyses through one, multimedia tool.

Join free for one month **library.macat.com**

Macat Disciplines

Access the greatest ideas and thinkers across entire disciplines, including

INEQUALITY

Ha-Joon Chang's, *Kicking Away the Ladder*
David Graeber's, *Debt: The First 5000 Years*
Robert E. Lucas's, *Why Doesn't Capital Flow from Rich To Poor Countries?*
Thomas Piketty's, *Capital in the Twenty-First Century*
Amartya Sen's, *Inequality Re-Examined*
Mahbub Ul Haq's, *Reflections on Human Development*

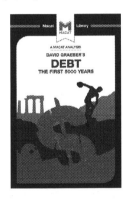

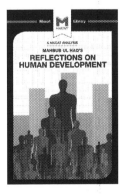

Macat analyses are available from all good bookshops and libraries.

Access hundreds of analyses through one, multimedia tool.
Join free for one month **library.macat.com**

Macat Disciplines

Access the greatest ideas and thinkers across entire disciplines, including

CRIMINOLOGY

Michelle Alexander's
The New Jim Crow: Mass Incarceration in the Age of Colorblindness

Michael R. Gottfredson & Travis Hirschi's
A General Theory of Crime

Elizabeth Loftus's
Eyewitness Testimony

Richard Herrnstein & Charles A. Murray's
The Bell Curve: Intelligence and Class Structure in American Life

Jay Macleod's
Ain't No Makin' It: Aspirations and Attainment in a Low-Income Neighborhood

Philip Zimbardo's
The Lucifer Effect

Macat analyses are available from all good bookshops and libraries.

Access hundreds of analyses through one, multimedia tool.

Macat Disciplines

Access the greatest ideas and thinkers across entire disciplines, including

Postcolonial Studies

Roland Barthes's *Mythologies*
Frantz Fanon's *Black Skin, White Masks*
Homi K. Bhabha's *The Location of Culture*
Gustavo Gutiérrez's *A Theology of Liberation*
Edward Said's *Orientalism*
Gayatri Chakravorty Spivak's *Can the Subaltern Speak?*

Macat analyses are available from all good bookshops and libraries.

Access hundreds of analyses through one, multimedia tool.
Join free for one month **library.macat.com**

Macat Disciplines

*Access the greatest ideas and thinkers
across entire disciplines, including*

GLOBALIZATION

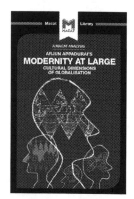

Arjun Appadurai's, *Modernity at Large:
Cultural Dimensions of Globalisation*

James Ferguson's, *The Anti-Politics Machine*

Geert Hofstede's, *Culture's Consequences*

Amartya Sen's, *Development as Freedom*

Macat analyses are available from all good bookshops and libraries.

Access hundreds of analyses through one, multimedia tool.

Join free for on~ ~~~th li~~~~ ~~~~ ~~~~~ ~ ~

Macat Pairs

Analyse historical and modern issues from opposite sides of an argument. Pairs include:

HOW TO RUN AN ECONOMY

John Maynard Keynes's
The General Theory OF Employment, Interest and Money

Classical economics suggests that market economies are self-correcting in times of recession or depression, and tend toward full employment and output. But English economist John Maynard Keynes disagrees.

In his ground-breaking 1936 study *The General Theory*, Keynes argues that traditional economics has misunderstood the causes of unemployment. Employment is not determined by the price of labor; it is directly linked to demand. Keynes believes market economies are by nature unstable, and so require government intervention. Spurred on by the social catastrophe of the Great Depression of the 1930s, he sets out to revolutionize the way the world thinks

Milton Friedman's
The Role of Monetary Policy

Friedman's 1968 paper changed the course of economic theory. In just 17 pages, he demolished existing theory and outlined an effective alternate monetary policy designed to secure 'high employment, stable prices and rapid growth.'

Friedman demonstrated that monetary policy plays a vital role in broader economic stability and argued that economists got their monetary policy wrong in the 1950s and 1960s by misunderstanding the relationship between inflation and unemployment. Previous generations of economists had believed that governments could permanently decrease unemployment by permitting inflation—and vice versa. Friedman's most original contribution was to show that this supposed trade-off is an illusion that only works in the short term.

Macat Disciplines

*Access the greatest ideas and thinkers
across entire disciplines, including*

THE FUTURE OF DEMOCRACY

Robert A. Dahl's, *Democracy and Its Critics*
Robert A. Dahl's, *Who Governs?*
Alexis De Toqueville's, *Democracy in America*
Niccolò Machiavelli's, *The Prince*
John Stuart Mill's, *On Liberty*
Robert D. Putnam's, *Bowling Alone*
Jean-Jacques Rousseau's, *The Social Contract*
Henry David Thoreau's, *Civil Disobedience*

Macat Disciplines

Access the greatest ideas and thinkers across entire disciplines, including

TOTALITARIANISM

Sheila Fitzpatrick's, *Everyday Stalinism*
Ian Kershaw's, *The "Hitler Myth"*
Timothy Snyder's, *Bloodlands*

Macat analyses are available from all good bookshops and libraries.

Access hundreds of analyses through one, multimedia tool.
Join free for one month **library.macat.com**